SHELF
SAINTS

SHELTERING SAINTS

LIVING WITH THE HOMELESS

ROGER QUICK

Illustrated by
SI SMITH

DARTON · LONGMAN + TODD

First published in 2022 by
Darton, Longman and Todd Ltd
1 Spencer Court
140 – 142 Wandsworth High Street
London SW18 4JJ

ISBN 978-1-913657-68-0

A catalogue record for this book is available from the British Library

Produced and designed by Judy Linard

Printed and bound by Bell & Bain, Glasgow

TO THOSE WHO HEAL

FOREWORD

Sleeping rough for just two days after a collapsed marriage was more than enough for me to realise that being homeless was rarely self-inflicted, and can so often induce feelings that no human being should ever have to endure. Helplessness, fear, despair and loneliness are just some of the unwanted baggage that comes with being homeless, and with suicidal thoughts so tragically common when there is no help around, I can only imagine why tragedies occur.

Thankfully people do pick themselves up and move forward, but it's never easy and so support and understanding are crucial in helping people who find themselves not only without a home but often losing their identity. That's why this second book from Father Roger Quick is so important to highlight the growing plight of the homeless, and should prick the conscience of everyone who reads it into understanding that they could be next ...

There is no immunity to homelessness.

Rick Wakeman CBE
Musician, songwriter, producer, presenter

INTRODUCTION

God give me a beautiful home. That is what a child wrote, having just learned about the work of St George's Crypt. We look after the people of Leeds who don't have any home, let alone a beautiful one. They come to us when there is nowhere left to go, no one else to turn to.

Like more than a third of my colleagues, I first came to the Crypt in need of help myself. Decades later I came back as its chaplain.

In 2021 we opened a block of 24 flats for our people, enabling them to move on from homelessness to a more stable life. We called it *Don Robins House*, after the young vicar who came to St George's Church in 1930 and founded the Crypt, moved by compassion to help the hundreds he saw tramping the streets and searching desperately for work during the Great Depression.

This is an account of the lives of some of those who have come to us over the last ninety-one years. Their

stories, like their lives, generally get forgotten. But they are important; to all of us in a society which allows such need to exist, and to those of us who try to follow the example of Jesus in living with the most despised and outcast people of his time. His life was by no means respectable; he made himself homeless, and tramped the streets, letting others feed and house him. He embarrassed his family. He knocked around with the wasters and losers of his day, and loved them.

Over the last eight years, I have been moved every day by the courage and insight, born of great suffering, that our people show. Everything has been against them. The unwanted children who grew into angry adolescents and disappointed adults; the vulnerable and damaged people who end up with us. Many of them have resorted to drugs or booze to numb the pain of their lives. Many of them – again like many of us – have had significant problems of mental health.

We reach out to their brokenness from our own.

These stories are true, and heart-breaking, and sometimes funny as well. There is a lot of laughter in the Crypt. Si Smith's beautiful illustrations have caught all of that, just as he did by freely providing his work in *Entertaining Saints*, the companion volume to this. All royalties go

to the work of the Crypt. By our friends' generosity and courage, we have been able to tell something of their lives. By the skill and encouragement of David Moloney and his exceptional staff at DLT, their stories have been given a voice. Chris Fields, chief executive of the Crypt, has supported and encouraged – as he always does – and given the time and space needed to record these stories.

Names and some details have been changed, except for those – too many – who have died; their lives deserve remembrance. We entrust them to the love of God, that all their hurt may be healed; that they may at last become everything they were meant to be; that they may rest in the peace so often denied them in this life, and rise in glory.

Pray for them all, and for us, as you read. We cannot do this work in our own strength.

Only by grace, only by love.

ONE STEP ENOUGH FOR ME

Memory is selective. When I turned up at the Crypt, having heard that they were looking for a chaplain, I had somehow managed to forget my first arrival there, thirty-odd years before. Gradually it came back to me. Like many of our people, I had had a violent domestic argument. And like many another verging alcoholic – in my case a binge-drinker who got hopelessly drunk every couple of weeks – I said to myself *I'll show her.* And so I set out deliberately to top up the very considerable amount I'd already had, and went out to get completely off my face.

Approaching midnight, I decided that going home wasn't an option. I asked a policeman if they would take me into the cells for the night. He laughed, and said I could try St George's Crypt – but they probably wouldn't have me in state I was in. And that was what happened; very kindly and gently, on my first appearance at the Crypt, I was turned away because I was too drunk. They said I could try the Salvation Army on Wellington Street. And so I made my unsteady way there. With more courtesy than I deserved, they too said they couldn't take me in because they were full; but suggested I try the men's Reception Centre on Whitehall Road. By now in the early hours, I set off across waste land, a building plot on what had been the old Leeds Central station. For some reason, quite suddenly, I stopped walking. Then I looked down. In front of me was a very deep hole in the ground; a couple of yards square. At the bottom, a long way down, I could see the moonlight reflecting off water. Two more steps and I would have fallen into it. If I had ever been found, it would have been too late. The shock of this sobered me up, to some extent. I walked to Headingley, looking for friends, and ended up sofa-surfing.

Many years later, I told this story to one of our friends in the Crypt; it seemed to me that he needed to know there was hope; that he wasn't forever locked in the life he was. Then, in case he thought I was just trying to look like one of the lads, I said, *But I wasn't much more than a student. I was just playing at it really.* He gave me a steady stare and said, *Oh, we could all say that.* He made me think again. Our homeless and vulnerable friends have taught me a lot. He was right. My life could have gone either way at that point; I could have ended up on the streets, or worse still might not have survived the night. It had been, in many ways, a turning point. Not long after I took a job as a church organist, needing even what small extra bit of money that would provide. What happened then is another story.

> *Lead kindly light, amid the encircling gloom…*
> *I do not ask to see the distant scene.*
> *One step enough for me.*

COMING BACK

I only knew the word furlough as applied to missionaries; after some years work in what was called the *mission field,* they would be granted time off back home. Presumably this was in part to stop them *going bush.* The other COVID word I had encountered only in prison: *Lockdown.* In prison, *full lockdown* means you have to stay wherever you happen to be: on the wing, in a cell, in chapel. This has led to some interesting (albeit long) conversations when visiting. Now we all know about Lockdown.

To comply with social distancing, all sorts of things changed in the Crypt. We couldn't use our beautiful chapel; our morning prayer together happened in the bigger space of the Assisi Café. Lunch there, usually a sit-down three-course meal for over a hundred, had to be swapped for a take-away walk-through meal, with guidelines taped to the floor. But still they came.

Like many of the Crypt staff, I contracted COVID early on, recovered gradually, and then was furloughed. Some of my colleagues worked straight through it all, with quiet courage, whatever the cost might be.

On my first day back, Felicity called me in to see Joel, remembering that I knew him twenty years ago, when he was a bright and lively lad. That child is barely recognizable now in the unwashed, drunken, barely coherent adult. He greets me warmly, as he always has, and tries to shake hands.

I try to conform to the rules: *Can't shake hands Joel; you don't know where I've been.* He looks confused and disappointed. Then asks me for a cross he can wear round his neck. When I come back with it, I hold it in his hands, having just sanitised mine, and pray a blessing, that it may be a sign of hope for him.

After some increasingly incoherent conversation, I go off on the next mission, leaving him with the indefatigably kind Felicity. But when she leaves him alone for a minute, Joel finds his way into the Crypt garden, and decides to help. For some reason his poor confused brain thinks that *helping* consists of pulling up plants and re-arranging the barriers we have put there to give people a safe passage through during the pandemic. Gently but firmly we ask him to go away and sober up. He wants to go to rehab, but insists he needs to go somewhere that will let him smoke: some places are harsher than others. I am not sure that he is ready even for this; but the likely alternative is that he will drink himself into an early grave.

The need has not gone away; some things haven't changed.

A BARNSLEY BLESSING

On my way to get a packet of cigs and a sandwich, I try to stay socially distanced from my fellow pedestrians. Then I get warmly embraced by every drunk on Great George Street, of whom there are surprisingly many this lunchtime. Two men (only slightly drunk) ask if I will pray with them, because they are off to Barnsley. Barnsley has an unfair reputation – a bit like where God chose to grow up: *Nazareth! Can anything good come from Nazareth?* (It did, but that's another story.)

We pray together, outside the pub. We pray that they might be welcomed joyfully, and safely return. Then Russian Sergei arrives, and also asks *You give blessing, yes?* The other two are delighted that they are not the only ones standing in the need of prayer.

On the way back wee Willy – who we haven't seen for a while – asks me for the blessing of a sleeping bag. I encourage him to come back to us; to get off the streets; to find somewhere warm and dry. He's just got out of hospital.

Then a young lady stops me and asks if we've got the Arts and Crafts today. Frankly I hadn't a clue, but Jamie was passing, and was able to tell her that it might be upstairs in the church. She was hoping for some lunch too, but has missed it. I consider giving her the cheese toastie I have in my bag; but she's talking to another lad by now, and I suspect he will want some as well, so leave them to it. If the old saying is true that you only get to keep in heaven what you've given away on earth, I've just missed out on a celestial cheese toastie. It didn't taste as nice as I thought it would, somehow.

PILGRIM

I went for a smoke after lunch, by the loading bay, as I often do. This has led to a lot of good conversations. I haven't met Colin before. He is clearly tense and nervous. A young man, he tells me he is just ten days into recovery from addiction, in one of our Growing Rooms houses. What's worrying him is his girlfriend; she is demanding more than he can give. He has enough on, trying to stay clean of drugs, without a stressful relationship. He says he's going to break up with her today. His accent isn't local. I ask where he's from. *Plymouth*. He doesn't look like one of the Pilgrim Fathers, but who knows? They must have had young men with them, and they certainly struggled (though perhaps in a different way) with sex and alcohol. He's worried that he should be back inside, working in the kitchen. I tell him he can use me as an excuse; tell them he's been talking to the Chaplain, who is known to witter on too much. He smiles and relaxes. We talk more; he pours his heart out, then says, *It's been like going into that little room where you talk to a priest.* Since he has made his confession already, I give him a blessing of absolution, cig in hand. Still valid. We need to know that we are forgiven; that a fresh start, beginning from where we are, is endlessly possible. It's all pilgrimage. *The Lord has put away your sin.* He takes a final deep drag and goes back inside, maybe a bit calmer.

DISTANCE

At the height of the pandemic, we looked after close on two hundred people every day and night. In the Crypt itself we had maybe twenty residents, all in separate rooms. Their meals are different from the usual melee. Carl has just finished lunch. Probably younger than thirty – our people tend to look older than they are – his thin dark hair is unwashed; he has a slight flush of sweat. Because of social distancing he has had to sit at a table by himself, well spaced-out from the others, as they all are. Our café looks like an exam room. I consider announcing that they can turn their papers over and begin; but few of our people like to be reminded of the consistent academic failure which marked their schooldays. Many – if not most – were troubled and excluded. Some were good at sport, but failed to fulfil their potential. Maybe they got in with the wrong crowd: soon enough they were the wrong crowd. Given a dysfunctional family, the need to belong can be desperate. Having to sit apart is not the least of the curses of the virus.

Our people are socially isolated at the best of times. Not only do they get lonely; they miss the reality-check that conversation with others can bring. And so they slide further down into their own dark places. I ask Carl if lunch was good. *Yeah. Yeah.* He half-laughs, and smiles to himself. He's clearly high on something. I'm not sure what this half-laugh means, but encounter it often enough. It's as though he's in conversation with an invisible third party who has just said to him, *What an idiot!* and he sniggered at the private joke. Yet even that has too much meaning. I doubt he could explain it himself.

CHOSEN

Poverty isn't just material. David tells me how he had arrived at primary school, aged eight, and after only a week had been sent to the headmaster. He thought he was in trouble yet again, but the head said to him, not unkindly: *Now then. You can't read can you?*

At this point in telling his story to me, David dropped his head in shame. *No, sir.*

Right. You're to come here to my office at the end of school every day. You'll be reading and writing by Christmas. And he was. He never forgot. But neither, clearly, did he forget the shame. Our people have everything stacked against them from the start. What is remarkable is the courage they somehow find to go on at all.

When I was a schoolmaster, I remember one day handing back some test papers. I didn't read out the results. As I handed one lad his, with a spectacularly poor result, I saw his look of resignation and failure; his shoulders drooped. He was no academic, and knew it, and was used to it. Then there came back to me an all too vivid memory of my own

schooldays. Playing sport, the teacher would choose two captains, who then chose their teams one by one. There would always be two left; the fat kid and me. That sense of failure, of rejection, of the impossibility of ever doing better, marked all of what it would be too optimistic to call my sporting career. For the first time (some of us are slow learners) I realized that for this child that same miserable, destroying, shaming experience didn't just happen once a week. It happened in every lesson.

Those who come to the Crypt have by definition failed in the class of life. We try to repair the damage. To give them hope in themselves. To let them know that they are valued; cherished. Each and only possessing the gift of being themselves.

Years ago, I said to a priest whose selfless and inspiring ministry I admired, *I wish I were more like you.* He smiled. *God's got one of me already.* We are given ourselves, which no one else can be. God knows who we are, and loves us for it.

FREEDOM

Edward is fragile. He is intelligent, articulate, sensitive, and living rough. He's come to us for food. There is a sense of brokenness about him; like a wounded bird. He tells me he wants to detox. I ask what he's on. Weed, Spice, Booze, and anything he's offered. Beggars can't be choosers. But he needs prescribed medication as well. He is registered with a medical practice some miles away. He can't afford the bus-fare to get that far, and isn't well enough to walk there and back. He needs to stay with us for a few nights, and get registered with the York Street medical practice, who look after our people wonderfully. Then he can get a diagnosis, and the meds he needs. Life can be exhausting.

That's one reason why a very few people actively choose to live on the streets. The administrative requirements of signing on for benefits, registering with the Housing Department, bidding for somewhere to live, regularly attending medical appointments, answering letters, having access to emails, having a bank account, keeping to a schedule, are just too much. Those who choose this hardest alternative of living rough are frequently troubled mentally. They are all – in my experience at least – deeply damaged; but the same could be said of some apparently successful captains of industry, who are just dealing with their problems in another way. Those determined to live on the street come to us for help from time to time, for a hot meal or clothing, alternating between what we can offer and how they want to live. Some see it as freedom.

THE BEST

P aul is sitting outside in his wheelchair. He's just finished lunch, and has two big empty paper cups. I offer to put them in the bin for him. He is really, genuinely grateful. I find myself moved by such thanks for so simple a thing, and by the fact that he is looking thinner; his wasting disease is beginning to take a more vicious toll. He wheels himself away, then calls over his shoulder as he rolls away, *Jesus is the best. He really is.*

Many of our people have a deep faith. Some respectable Churches maintain that addicts can't be Christians. Addiction to material possessions apparently doesn't count. We might deny that we are addicts; but just try giving up the things you enjoy most. Try giving up a new car, or nice curtains or matching bedding. Try giving up a nice meal out with the family. Try giving up a bigger telly or a faster computer or a new mobile. It's hard. I know because I don't manage it either. And so we look around and tell ourselves it's all right because everyone else is doing it. Giving things away can help. Don't ask yourself, *Will I need this again?* Ask yourself, *Could someone else use this?* We don't have to do without it all at once, though in the end we will. Practising helps: being truly thankful heals.

Many of us, afflicted by poverty, homelessness, a painful terminal disease, could feel like cursing God. Paul doesn't. Some weeks later, he tells me he is doing better, putting on weight, still in his wheelchair. He is thankful. *Jesus is the best. He really is.*

LIGHT IN THE DARKNESS

Lucas is sitting on the back step of the loading bay. He's not smoking, which is generally why people go there. He is sitting on the ground, bowed forward, looking utterly miserable. I ask how he's doing. Not good. He's just done rehab, and is coming off methadone, the heroin substitute which can be as difficult to let go of as the drug itself. He is frightened and close to despair. *I feel like I just want to run away from myself.* Many of us know that feeling only too well. I wish I knew better what to say. Today he has volunteered to work in the kitchens. It can be a comfort – or at least a distraction – to lose yourself in whatever the next task is; peeling potatoes, washing up – anything really. Meister Eckhart says that the answer is *to do the next thing you have to; doing it with all your heart; and finding joy in it.*

I remember I have a new cross in my pocket, and ask if he would like one. Even if he doesn't pray much, just wearing some physical reminder can help, can encourage; to hope, to believe in himself and maybe the God whose love has never abandoned him. Who is with him in his sorrow. No one has ever refused; no one is ever turned away. I undo the plastic bag, and let it fall into his outstretched hand, then give the words of blessing, that it may be a sign to him of light in the darkness. It will. It's luminous. He'll find that out sometime after midnight. May the light be a blessing to him.

JEDI

Liam has collected his soup and gone through to have it outside, as social distancing requires. This might have been pleasant in summer, but is less so as October turns towards winter. Then he sits on the wall and takes his shoe and sock off. He has a nasty blister on his heel. *Have you got any trainers?* My heart sinks. Having looked in the cupboard earlier, he'll be lucky.

Size 8 or 9. I can fit either. And some socks if you've got any. Please.

There is a note of desperation. Footwear matters a lot when you're tramping the streets.

I go to have a look. As I thought, there are no trainers. In fact there are only four pairs of shoes, and two of them are size 7. I take the other two pairs out; just in case. With almost as much regret as I offer them, he politely declines. I know why. If you were joining friends for lunch in one of the leafier northern suburbs, these snakeskin loafers would ideally match a pair of light flannels and a golfing jersey. Three days on the hard wet streets of Leeds and they'd fall apart. At least I was able to find him a couple of pairs of decent socks. His thanks is generous, given that we had no suitable footwear.

Back inside, I suddenly remember that I have a packet of plasters in my drawer, and run back outside, thinking they might ease his blister. He's gone already; maybe back on the trainer trail. At which point another of our friends comes up. Andy looks at me suspiciously. Come to think of it, he always does. I don't think he means anything by it; his face is just stuck like that. Maybe the wind changed direction. As one of the more popular prophets of a long time ago said, far, far away:

Your eyes can deceive you. Don't trust them. Meanwhile, back at base:

Have you got a first-aid box?

Not wanting to answer yes, in case he wants the whole box, nicks off with it and flogs the paracetamol on the street as something else, I ask what he needs. *I need a first-aid box!*

This could clearly go round in circles. Indeed, it already has, and his short fuse is fast burning out. Then I remember what I'm carrying in my hand. *Do you want some plasters?*

He looks as relieved as I feel. *Yeah! Have you got some?*

I offer him four Star Wars plasters. He contemplates them, then chooses the Darth Vader one, in case someone else likes Wookiees, which is kind. *You can have them all. You'll need another one later.*

He is thrilled. More than a few plasters really warrant. Maybe he's a Jedi Knight underneath. Most people are, if you look hard enough.

THE PRESENT

You wouldn't think it was too difficult to keep track of a cross on a necklace, especially if you wear it round your neck. But somehow Theresa manages to lose them. Where they go is a mysterious imponderable. It is said that the odd sock is the larval form of the spare coat-hanger, thus accounting for the large incidence of both. What a cross might hatch out into is less clear. I tell her that if she loses this one, more are always available. Praying a blessing as I give it her, I include a blessing on whoever has found the last one. We often find ourselves praying for people we have lost. Most of our residents stay for a week or so, and then move on; into housing provided by the Council; or they just slip away. This has gone on at the Crypt for over ninety years now.

We meet so many people; in shops, at work, or just passing on the street. Their lives all have a story. Fleetingly our lives intersect, and each meeting gives us the possibility to make their lives better or worse. A few years ago, I suffered a disabling illness. Going to the supermarket was only manageable on a good day. Whoever was on the checkout would likely be the only person I would meet that day. If they were pleasant and friendly, the day was better; if they were sullen and grumpy it was worse. How they behaved for those few moments could change the colour of the whole day.

I haven't forgotten that. I took it as an encouragement to value everyone who comes to us; fragile, hurting, chaotic, or just given to losing crosses. We only have to live the gift of the now. That's why it's called the present.

HOUSE BEAUTIFUL

We talk to many different groups about our work at the Crypt, and try to match the message to the audience. (Or, in the case of our occasional visits to Spiritualist churches, the message to the medium.) In prosperous areas, we tell the stories of those who have come to us whose lives were comfortable and apparently secure, until some crisis overwhelmed them; lawyers and lecturers have sometimes found themselves homeless.

In schools, where the compassion of children is always moving, we sometimes tell the stories of children abandoned by their parents; of more than one who ran away from home, whose parents never looked for them; who grew up unloved and unwanted; who ended up with us as adults, damaged and hurting.

The day following one such visit, as we gather for morning prayer, Chris hands out some cards we have received from a primary school. Each of them has a prayer written by one of the pupils. They have imagined well the things they would miss if they were homeless. One simply said, *God give me a beautiful home.*

A good home is what any of us aspires to. A beautiful home goes further, and imagines a place of delight; a place of joy, of love, of reconciliation, of laughter, of hope and harmony.

Maybe also a place of healing tears, to keep it real (which beauty surely must be). A place of safety, of clean sheets and good food lovingly prepared. A place with other people who love you, and whom you can love – what would be the point of having a beautiful house if there were no one else to delight in it? Bunyan would surely approve.

FREE FLOWERS

Sometimes our people find it hard to feel forgiven. Guilt and shame were battered into them as children; forgiveness was rare.

We don't need to *deserve* love. It's just there. It's just here. And everything in us can fight against it. We want to control the deal. We want to deserve what we get, and we never can. Love unmerited and free. It is here. *For where two or three are gathered in my name, I am there among them.* What does that mean: *Gathered in my name?* Well it doesn't just mean when we claim to be Christians. That would include the atrocities of the Inquisition and the brutalities exacted under Cromwell. It means *wherever two or three people act lovingly.* Then, and only then, and always then, the Spirit of God is there. And when they don't act lovingly? When *we* don't? Jesus is there too. Suffering with us in our resentment and fear and anger, or crucified by our smugness.

Some years ago, I knew a dear lady who was in charge of flower-arranging for weddings. (A dangerous calling if ever there was one). And whenever I gave her phone number to a couple who were making arrangements for their wedding, it was with some trepidation. In the end I took to saying to them something like, *She might seem a bit gruff, but her bark is worse than her bite.* This was not necessarily true; but I thought it might help them to think that it was. Either way, it gave her the benefit of the doubt. She was, as her friends would point out, a tireless worker for the church. And I remember one Saturday we had two weddings. The second one was a poor couple, on a tight budget. After the first wedding, I found her moving the flowers out of church into the vestry.

Why not just leave them for the next wedding? I said.

29

But they haven't paid for them! she said. *Why should I leave them?*

What struck me then was how angry she was. Furiously, deeply, bitterly angry. And that can be a good sign. Too often Christians try too hard to be *nice*. Too often we replace an honest, more courageous love, with the infinitely weaker *niceness*.

There is a saying that *no man is angry but first he is hurt.*

Why should I leave them? They haven't paid for them.

She glared at me; hurting and angry and zealous for justice.

Because God's love is free. Let it be a sign to them of that.

She put them back. We got on better after that.

REAL MIRACLES

Not a day goes by in the Crypt when I don't thank God that as a child I knew I was loved. From that foundation anything is possible. Too many of our people never had that.

They began as unwanted, accidental babies, whose mothers don't know what to do with them because they themselves were never given the love they needed. They turned into unruly and angry toddlers, and a lot of them stayed that way. They arrived at school, not knowing the names of colours: sometimes they didn't know their own name. Desperate for the attention they never had, they got it in school by imitating the violent and disruptive behaviour they saw at home.

So they struggled in class; they became bitter and rebellious teenagers; they left school unqualified and hopeless. Desperate to be loved, they made use of the only asset they had – the beauty of youth – and passed relentlessly from one relationship to another, hoping to find the love they never had, from others who all too often were as confused and desperate and angry as themselves.

Then suddenly they are adults, and our society holds them accountable for everything they do and are.

Don't judge anyone until you've walked a mile in their shoes. To which one of our friends added, with the dark humour which keeps us going in the Crypt, *because by then you're a mile away and you've got a new pair of shoes.*

As I listen to their stories,

heart-breaking and all too predictable, often enough I will say, *That's a reason but it's no excuse.* We don't do anyone any favours by telling them it's not their fault. Of course it isn't. But we need to know that we have choice; that we have agency. That what we choose to do *now* will make a difference. This is empowering; the other is dispiriting.

Sometimes, talking to Churches, whose support is vital to us – in prayer as in more obviously practical ways – I get asked, *What miracles have you seen?* And I want to answer that it is a miracle that our people are walking and talking, holding what looks like a normal conversation. Because inside they are terrified children; longing for love they never had.

So what do we do? We welcome them. Where we get it right, we welcome them as though we've been looking out for them, hoping they would come. We give them a good hot meal. We give them somewhere safe and warm and dry to sleep. By the generosity of those who give to us, we give them clean underwear and warm clothing. And we listen to their stories, and answer their need to pray if they ask for it. And see in every face the face of Jesus, however cunningly disguised.

COME AGAIN

Often, when talking with the families of someone who has died, I will ask them what they think happens when you die. And sometimes, if they trust me enough, someone will say *Well no one's ever come back to tell us, have they?*

A strange thing to say to a professional Christian. If someone did come back from death to tell us, wouldn't we do everything in our power to tell the whole world? That is what I believe happened in AD33. Something happened which turned Jesus' disciples from a terrified huddle, hiding away in case they met the same fate, into people willing to risk their lives in order to tell everyone that very thing: that Jesus of Nazareth, who everyone knew had died, had come through death to life; had *come back to tell us*. That is the heart of the Gospels. Anything else follows from that. The rest is contingent. What mattered was the Resurrection. And that changes everything.

It changes the meaning of our lives here and now. If this life were all there is; if I saw so many of our friends in the Crypt living inexpressibly painful lives, dying young and desperately unfulfilled, then there would be every reason to despair. But there isn't. There is hope. And that hope

33

is rooted in the constant, eternal, indefatigable, incapable of disappointment, love of God.

And if all this were to turn out to be an illusion, a story to comfort children frightened of the dark? I think all of us who work at St George's Crypt would say that our lives have been better for having lived believing it to be true. Infinitely better.

FALLING

One of our residents has hanged himself. My colleagues who found him are understandably shocked. Inevitably, desperately, we ask *why?* In this case, though not always, we know something of the circumstances. He had been abusing his partner; when she left, he had nowhere else to direct his anger, and so turned it on himself. Such a twisted logic seems believable in this case. His partner is now staying with us, beside herself with grief and guilt, taking refuge in any sort of drug which can numb the pain and help her forget.

His family did not want her to attend the funeral. So we arranged to have a memorial service after lunch on Tuesday. We got ready, and lit a candle. She came in, sat on a chair and fell off it. We managed to catch her before she hit the floor, laid her down in the recovery position, and phoned an ambulance. It looked like Spice; but we knew she didn't like Spice. Then we learn that maybe one of our other residents might have given it her so that he could rob her, or worse. We watched and waited and prayed. The candle shone, steadily and silently. By the time the paramedics arrived, she was conscious again, and could be trusted – more or less – to sit on a chair. The man whom we suspect gave her the drugs looked round the door to wish her all the best.

She decided to postpone the service till next week. Her social worker came again, travelling in from another part of the city. We re-lit the candle, said some prayers, and read a poem she had written; startling in the rawness of its grief; clinging desperately to the hope of some better life after this.

NIGHTMARE

Father Darren gives me a call and asks me to look out for Dermot, who is a devout heroin addict. Some people don't believe that drug addicts can be Christians. These people are usually those who are so unsure of their own forgiven-ness that they need to condemn other more obvious sinners. We are all addicted to something; money, television, tidiness, sex, the approval of others, Church. Christ, have mercy. Being addicted means not being able to cope without your drug of choice. Try weaning yourself off it. If you can't sit comfortably until you've polished the carpet and swept the sunlight, force yourself to sit down in the mess and not clear it up for a day. Don't do the washing-up. Don't shower. Live like that *just for today*. That's how hard it is to give up heroin. Times one hundred.

Dermot is doing it. Somehow, against all the odds, after years of addiction, he has stayed clean of drugs for a week. Longing to use every waking moment. Hearing the little voice saying, *Just once will be all right. One last time*. But he knows he can't. Because he's caught the vision of something better. He's now living in a shared house with three other recovering addicts. It is warm and comfortable; he can take a hot shower and wear clean clothes. Most of all, he's found a purpose in life, and an aim. He wants to get back home; to see his brothers and sisters again.

But last night he was frightened. He had a nightmare. In the dream he used heroin again, and was suffering the after-effects. Not just the physical things, which are bad enough; in the dream he was suffering all the guilt and shame. He'd done it again. He'd let himself down, and everyone else. He was never going to be any different. In the dream his brother came to him and laid into him every which way. He was wasting his life and he needed to stop or he'd be dead. Then he woke up; in a cold sweat because he thought he'd used again. And then the relief flooded over him. It was just a dream.

But now, hours later, the dream was still haunting him. In desperation he sought me out. He needed help to pray. We all do, sometimes. He needed an angel of the agony to be beside him in his Gethsemane. We prayed, and wept, and thanked God it was only a dream, and brought him back to his tenuous, hopeful reality.

Carrots, Broccoli & Shrooms

Gareth tells me that one of our clients was disappointed on tasting our mushroom soup.

Our very creative chefs can make a tasty meal out of anything. Once we were donated six large sacks of walnuts. When I asked what could be made of them, the reply immediately came back: *Waldorf Salad!* Getting our guys to eat anything green is often a bit of a struggle. When you've been roughing it on the streets, getting your five a day is not really a priority. We do what we can by providing a nourishing and varied three-course meal.

Recently, Dr Lasana Harris conducted some interesting research in London. He found that when people were shown pictures of someone begging, their brains reacted as they would on being shown an object, not a person. That is how far we dehumanize those in need; we literally don't see them as people. Then he found that this reaction could be reversed, by asking the observer whether they thought the person begging would prefer carrots or broccoli. Sometimes it's that simple. Being vulnerable enough to put yourself in their place. Empathy.

Today, however, our friend was disappointed by the soup. This was the more surprising, since it was made from scratch using fresh mushrooms. We always listen to our customers' preferences: carrots or broccoli for example. Today's request was less easily met; apparently our friend had been hoping for *magic* mushroom soup, and was waiting for the effects of the shrooms to kick in.

Now, although psilocybin have been used in many religious traditions across the world, we had to tell him that Church of England was not one of them. Unless of course that admirable organisation the Mothers' Union has updated its recipe book in some very unexpected ways.

FLEEING THE DRAGON

Paul has asked me to phone him. A recovering addict, he has been struggling these last few weeks. He tells me that it is the last ten percent that is the hardest. All the rest he's managed; that itself is an extraordinary achievement. The courage of those who battle against addiction is inspiring. Who knows what small changes in our own lives could have led any of us to that dark place. Paul is a devout Christian, and has made one corner of his bedsit into a place for prayer.

The thing is: he didn't expect this last part to be the hardest, the most painful. He thought that, having come so far, this would be the easiest. But it is one of the hardest. We don't tell people that at the outset; they are going to find the journey hard enough, without knowing what's round the corner. It is one of the mercies of time that we do not have to do everything at once. This, at least, I can tell him. It's not just one day at a time; it's one *moment* at a time.

The depth of the pain surprises him. He tells me it's like his skin has been ripped off.

I tell him the story of Eustace. C. S. Lewis's unlovely character becomes a dragon as a result of his greed. Eventually, Aslan frees him from the curse by stripping off his dragon's skin.

This is incredibly painful; but underneath is a new, and fresh, and wonderfully *human* skin. Sometimes it feels like that.

Sometimes stories written for children are the ones that tell us the truth, and heal the little child under the dragon we have become.

CROSSED OFF

I get asked to say a few words of encouragement, a prayer and blessing on a video for us to post online for Christmas. This seems straightforward enough, and I am glad to have the opportunity to ask for the prayers of the many who support us. Whatever we do is enabled by prayer; truly. We can't do it in our own strength.

After it goes online, one of my more fervently Christian colleagues comes to me, unsure how her fellow Calvinists will react to the video. I try to remember some heresy I have innocently promulgated. (Or rather, which in my utter depravity I was predestined to commit.) Nothing struck me as hideously offensive to the Elect. Then she told me:

The blessing. You made the sign of the cross!

Ah. Yes. In a Catholic church, the priest asks God's blessing upon the Faithful by making the sign of the cross, and they acknowledge this by crossing themselves. In many Anglican churches, the priest makes the sign of the cross, and gets faithfully ignored. In some Protestant traditions, the minister raises both arms (a bit like Superman but without taking off. Usually.) I'm not sure what happens in her church. I imagine most people have their eyes closed (or are supposed to anyway) so you'd think it wouldn't matter; but I guess watching a video inclines one to keep eyes open even in prayer. And my making a sign of the cross would have divided us, rather than united. Truly sorry to have offended my brethren and cistern, I am also – may I be forgiven – giggling a bit as well.

Next Christmas I'll sit on my hands. Cross my heart and hope to die.

BIBLE READINGS

I know my Bible. The lady is in her forties (probably), swaying slightly, surrounded by a halo of beer fumes. *I know my Bible! Do you know how it starts and ends?*

I wait, suspecting that this may be a slightly different reading.

Don't Give ... and Don't Take!

For a moment I struggle to reconcile this with the infinite generosity with which Genesis begins, and the absolute hope at the end of Revelation. Then I give up, and say – in what I trust is a voice of gentle encouragement – *Isn't that wonderful!*

The point is, she thinks it's wonderful. Somehow, somewhere in her poor addled brain there is a sense that Scripture contains good things. For the moment, she needs to know herself loved, accepted. Then she asks if she can have some bedding. I have to say no, since we struggle to launder bedding for up to fifty people a night in the Crypt. And, frankly, we want to encourage people to come inside rather than sleep on the streets. She accepts my refusal with that quiet resignation we so often see in those for whom disappointment has become the norm. It breaks my heart, every time. *There might just be a chance. I'll go and look.*

I have half a memory that a few weeks ago I found what looked like a new sleeping bag, and squirrelled it away. Miraculously, it was where I'd left it. I hid it in a carrier bag, and took it to her. She asked if I'd got another for her friend, who has toothache. Unfortunately I have neither more bedding nor analgesics. *Thanks anyway love. I know my Bible.*

Sometimes the rules get bent; I had given, she had taken, and as always vice-versa. We receive more than we give, immeasurably. The Bible tells us so.

Unusual treatment

Having an office next to the back door of the Crypt is not always convenient. Our guests know that they should go to the front, where we can welcome them, sign them in, and so keep a charitable eye on who's in the building. The back door is where we gratefully unload donations, or load up the van. No one is on permanent back-door duty; like many other tasks in the Crypt it's just a case of whoever is around. On this occasion a repeated knocking was not immediately answered so I went. Not, it must be admitted, with very good grace. I was probably writing a sermon, or on my way from Jericho to Jerusalem. Nor did I remember to greet the rather ragged man as though it was Jesus dropping in. Only English politeness stopped me from interrupting as he told his labyrinthine tale. Eventually even good manners ran out, and I asked him what he wanted. A cup of tea. I told him that if he went round the front, he could get a full lunch. He didn't want to do that, because he was *Restricted* from the Crypt. *I was smoking because I had pneumonia.* An unusual treatment. *In my room.* Ah. Residents are welcome to go out for a cig, but are not encouraged to smoke, drink or shoot up inside. I suggested he asked to have his restriction lifted. This is possible, given some sign of repentance, which I am not, frankly, seeing at the moment. *What happens if they say no?* I am inclined to say that he should have thought of that before he broke the rules. In any case, I suspect there is much more to his story than he's letting on, and end our conversation. Maybe next time. We live in hope; that's what we're here for.

GROWING UP

Jason hailed me warmly; I confess I did not immediately recognize him. He tells me he remembers me from my parish, many years ago. Gradually, I have a flicker of remembrance. He was a lively lad; maybe a bit troubled, but not so much that I would have predicted the course his life has evidently taken. I can't bring myself yet to ask him what went wrong. Whatever it was has brought him to a chronic dependence on drink and drugs. It is hard to see the bright, lively boy under the ravaged face here now; unwashed, missing teeth, his speech slurred. Maybe in due course he will tell me his story. Maybe not. That is for him to share if he wants to. In the meantime we can offer him food, somewhere warm and safe to stay, and the assurance that he matters. He asks me for a cross. That, at least, we can supply. We pray together. Afterwards, I feel gutted. It is the loss of hope; the disappointment of all he could have been.

I knew that back then his family was troubled, to say the least. So much so that he was often taken in by a kind lady from Church, whose own problems were considerable, as is

often the way. Our own grief, used rightly, makes us softer to the griefs of others. And if Jason chooses one day to tell me all his story of neglect, abuse, violence and disappointment, I will tell him that he still has the capacity to make good decisions, and change, however gradually. To become everything that he was created to be. To have hope that that bright and lively boy is not lost forever.

44

YORKSHIRE HALLELUJAH

Not long after I started as chaplain, the American evangelist Tony Campolo came to preach at St George's Church, above the Crypt. I had been persuaded by the Spirit to go, despite harbouring a constitutional suspicion of evangelists in general, and of overly slick Americans in particular. (This despite my own dear evangelist grandfather having been Saved in Kalamazoo.) We may hope to be forgiven.

Tony confirmed my prejudices by beginning with a shouted *Hallelujah!* This was greeted with a muffled and slightly embarrassed congregational *Hallelujah.* He looked around us all and said, *You're English, aren't you.* With that one line he had me. We collapsed in thankful laughter. He was acknowledging a cultural difference. This was not going to be an absolutist sermon. I listened, and loved it, and was blessed. The world was in darkness; but *that's because it's Friday.* We stood together at the foot of the Cross. *But Sunday's coming!* He spoke of hope in the darkness. And that Hope stayed with me in the days and years to come at the Crypt.

When Prince Harry was to be married, it was announced that the American bishop Michael Curry was to preach. A week before, I did a quick search on the internet to find out who he was. Two hours later I emerged, inspired and encouraged by his preaching. (Contrary to general perception, clergy do not spend all their downtime watching other people's sermons.)

The next day, before Grace at lunchtime, I asked our friends in the Crypt to pray for Bishop Michael as he prepared to preach to the biggest congregation on Earth. Then I sent a message to his staff to say that the homeless people of Leeds were holding him in their prayers. The next day, I was able to share a reply; that he was praying for us too.

We were not disappointed. Bishop Michael turned out to be the surprise hit of the show. Two days later, the Crypt was buzzing with it. *That was him we were praying for, right?*

And he were praying for us and all?

Yes, he was.

Well he did all right. (Highest praise. This is Yorkshire.) *I mean, he were fantastic!*

His friend wasn't so sure. *Yeah, but he went on a bit.*

No he didn't! It were about love, right? Well we all need a bit more of that.

Yeah. Right. Fair enough is that. For which read, *Amen, brother.* We had our Hallelujahs.

THIS NEW DAY

E very morning the Crypt gathers at 9 o'clock for prayer; in our beautiful chapel, or when social distancing demands it, in our Assisi Cafe. It takes a while for us all to arrive; people are always the priority. We talk about what concerns us, then offer it in prayer; sometimes cautiously, since our prayers have often been answered in great abundance. Prayers for towels once resulted in a delivery of twelve boxes. Just coincidence of course. We follow a regular pattern; opening lines and responses, then the psalm of the day.

The set reading – often from the Gospels – follows. Then we consider it together, seeing how it speaks to us in the Crypt for that day; how we can live out this good news. Then we pray for all those we care for; for those in particular need; for one another; for the wider world and in thanks for the gift of life, for the universe, for the unimaginable aeons of existence. This is extempore, spontaneous prayer; not all my colleagues come from traditions comfortable with set words. I am grateful that they put up with the chaplain's funny little ways. We end with the *Our Father,* a Collect and a blessing. All quite normal really. And yet extraordinary; remembering why we do what we do. We sit beneath paintings of those gathered at the Last Supper; paintings of our residents. They remind us to see the saint in all of those who come through our doors, and in our colleagues.

Does it get boring saying the same words day after day? Sometimes. But that is temporary; we come through the other side into a place where the words have become part of us. They live in us, and shape what we do and who we are. *Rejoicing in the gift of this new day.*

GEORGE AND THE DRAGON

Not long after I started as chaplain to the Crypt we took in a young man – perhaps thirty – who came from one of the rural parts of Yorkshire. Tall and well built, George was a drinker. Farming is notoriously difficult these days; compared with the population as a whole, farmers are twice as likely to commit suicide. George was evidently troubled; we went into our lovely chapel to talk. He told me about his childhood. His mother had died young, leaving just him and his father. He told me that his dad would go to the pub every night. *But whatever time he got home – it might be 11 o'clock or whenever – he'd get on and cook us dinner. Every night!* There was no hint of reproach; quite the opposite. He loved his dad.

The next morning I saw George again, by our front desk. He was already drunk. Drunk and desperate. With tears flowing down his face he cried out to me, *I want to stop! It's like I've got a devil inside me. Help me!*

My heart went out to him, poor lad. I heard what he said.

Do you want rid of it?

Yes. Yes! Help me!

It was like watching a man

49

drown. Without stopping to think, I threw out the only lifeline I knew, placed a hand on his chest and told the devil that had hold of him to go and not come back. This came as much of a surprise to me as to him – to George, that is – though possibly to his demon as well. We both broke down in tears, and hugged each other. He needed a hug. And so, to be honest, did I. He dried his tears, and smiled.

The next day he came to me. *I don't know what you did, but it's worked. I haven't even felt like a drink.* He looked a lot better. In fact, he looked good. He looked happy.

Well, thank God for that then. We prayed together a brief prayer of thanks, and hope.

Within a few days, he had moved on. Still dry, still thankful.

There is a protocol for what is called the Ministry of Deliverance. People get very excited about demonic possession. Horror films have a lot to answer for; atheists can end up believing in vampires and zombies. But Possession is a rare and specific thing. Oppression by evil seems more often encountered. The protocol would have required me to contact the diocesan minister with responsibility for such things; to have had two of us present, and be surrounded by the prayer of the faithful. All of that is good; on this occasion there just wasn't time. This child of God needed help there and then and by grace, I believe, received it.

The miracle was doubled, in that I am not sure of what I believe in all this. And that despite C. S. Lewis's dictum, that the two errors the human race can fall into about devils are either not to believe in them, or to take an unhealthy exaggerated interest in them. But as my tutor at Mirfield would say, *Well I expect God got round it somehow.* He does that a lot. In the end, credal dogmatics was not the issue. George needed help. By grace, he received it. We never saw him again. We pray for him still, and are thankful.

BUT NOW I SEE

R ocky was one of our regulars. She so much loved the character played by Sylvester Stallone that she took his name. She still identified herself as female, though would occasionally dress as a man. Her choice entirely. (I myself often wear a long white frock, having a liking for the traditional priestly vestments.)

Her life had not been easy; being a working girl on the streets had taken its toll on the fragile and sensitive soul who was still evident under the butch bravado. She regularly attended any services we held. Rather than impose a hymn on them, I would ask for requests. Too often the Church requires that others conform to our worship, rather than acknowledging the presence of God in the lives of everyone.

Her request was always the first, and always the same: *Amazing Grace*. The hymn of a reformed slave-trader speaks powerfully to our people of hope in the midst of the storms of life. After this had gone on for some time, I asked if she wouldn't like to sing something else. Even our limited hymnbook – nicknamed *Cheery Tunes for Cheerful Christians* – has a moderate variety. Her reply caught me off guard:

No! I know that one and I can't read.

Had I taken time to notice, I might have guessed. Too many of our people have had an education at best patchy. Adults who are illiterate have shown courage and resourcefulness in somehow hiding it, or getting round it.

So we sang John Newton's hymn again, with a renewed and enlightened understanding. It will never be the same for us, no matter how many times we sing it:

We've no less days to sing God's praise than when we first begun.

ST MARCELO

The whole point about saints is that they are human. Turning them into something else doesn't do them – or us – any favours. The difficulty comes in recognizing the saints living around us. Like many clergy, I have conducted hundreds of funerals, mostly for people I have never known. Never once have I heard a family's account of the loved one they have lost without wishing I could have met them.

Joe is from Eastern Europe. Exactly where, he is reluctant to say. When your country has been riven by war, conflict or genocide, even mentioning the name can be painful. He may also be protecting those he had to leave behind. He tells me he is from Leeds now, and wears a Leeds United cap all the time to prove it. That helps him make friends, me included. We talk about recent matches, and about the proud history of Elland Road. It always means more than the game; if the definition of a sacrament really is *an outward and visible sign of an inward and spiritual grace*, then that too might just include football, whose particular grace at its best has to do with belonging: *Marching on together.* Belonging, and hope, and glory. Sometimes it comes even closer than that to the faith we affirm: the head coach of Leeds, himself a devout Catholic, knows how it works:

> *Whoever is loved will always feel safer, and have that sensation of strength that puts him in a better position to confront the battle....*
>
> *You have to really love the people you're leading; and if you don't really feel it, you've got to learn how.*

Well said, Marcelo Bielsa.

BLESS THIS HOUSE

The Crypt had bought a new house. When funding was withdrawn for our old dry house, Faith Lodge, we needed an alternative, and developed our *Growing Rooms*. Houses with four men in each, all in recovery from addiction of various sorts, taking part in a carefully worked-out programme; encouraging one another. In the end we had a few houses; good, solid Victorian terraces, in one of the least expensive parts of Leeds. The lads themselves helped us to clear them out, renovate and redecorate. Then we would have a house blessing.

All buildings; houses, churches, brothels, sometimes seem to retain a memory of what has happened in them. Everyone who comes into our chapel at the Crypt is aware of its spirit, which many describe simply as *Peace*. Prayer seems to seep into the walls; but so can the bad stuff.

Whatever the objective reality, giving thanks for a new home is always good.

For a house blessing, we gather together, generally starting in the kitchen, which is so often the hub of a home. I like to use the old words for blessing holy water, and to do so there and then, so that everyone is involved. Beginning by thanking God for this new shared life, we move together from room to room, blessing each one, and every space and stairway and cupboard from bottom to top, praying that everywhere may be a place of love, and peace, and laughter and joy and healing. The laughter is important, and we laugh a lot in the midst of blessing.

One house in particular had a bit of a problem. I knew that it had somehow missed out on the house-blessing. Maybe the lads did too. One or two of them had become convinced of the presence of evil in the cellar. *Evil* is a funny word; a bit like *darkness*. We know that darkness is nothing

54

but the absence of light, but it's useful to have a word for it.

We gathered together in the kitchen, blessed the water, and then immediately went down together to the cellar.

It seemed to me there was an air of sadness there; although I am not particularly sensitive to these things. But I reminded everyone of all the good things that would surely have happened in the cellar; a mother lovingly doing the washing for her family, with a posser and scrubbing board and mangle. We thanked God for that loving service, and blessed every space, and – almost incidentally – prayed that those who had lived before us in this place might rest in peace.

Then we went together through the whole house, praying for refreshing sleep in the bedrooms; for shared laughter in the living room; for a spirit of welcome at the front door: *the Lord will watch over your going out and coming in....*

With a final blessing we were done. I stood in the hallway, and thought of the family who had lived there when the house was built. I was overcome by a sense of joy and light, and must have said something, because one of the lads asked if I was talking to someone. *Might have been.* It was a truthful answer, and a happy one.

The problems they had experienced resolved. Not quite immediately; grace works in God's good time; we all get to share in turning from darkness to light. All blessings.

FIGHT THE GOOD FIGHT

Nigel was keen on football. Though not so much the game itself as fighting violently with the other side's supporters. He tells me that's all in the past now. I find it hard to imagine this cheerful hard-working man going to Elland Road on a Saturday afternoon just to get into a fight. He didn't really know why; he just enjoyed the high it gave him. But sometimes a shadow would cross his face – of anger or frustration – which made it easier to see the suppressed aggression beneath. He was nervous, and alcoholic, albeit high-functioning; it wasn't obvious. Some people hide it very well.

Many of those who come to us for help are in addiction, or have been, or are struggling to get free of it. Their addictions take many forms, but at root seem to be about escaping something or numbing the pain: rarely about just experiencing pleasure. The adrenaline rush of fighting works the same way. And football hooliganism offers a sense of camaraderie, however misplaced.

Belonging, like any virtue, can be corrupted. The dark side cannot create; it can only corrupt. Look at any spectacular wickedness, and you will find something good which has been perverted. Love of country; eating; sex; all great and good things until they are grossly indulged, and turn into extreme nationalism, gluttony or sexual violence. The good may be rediscovered; maybe Nigel will one day watch United for the sheer joy of it.

LOVED

Bella came to us from the Glasgow tenements. It was a tough place to grow up in the 1950s, and her lined and tired face showed what it had cost her. Her childhood was one of neglect and abuse. She had married young, like so many, to get away from what passed for home, and found only that she had swapped one drunken and violent man for another. Eventually she escaped down south, and ended up in Leeds, where life had been little kinder to her, and she ended up in the Crypt. She put a brave face on it all.

One day we got talking. Shyly and hesitantly, she told me she had not been baptized as a child. She felt ashamed. Just one more way in which she had fallen short, been left out, excluded. When I told her we could put that right, she lit up. *Are you serious? Could I still have it at my age?*

We could do it today, if you wanted.

This was maybe too much for her.

Can I have a think about it?

We talked some more; about what this could mean; about turning away from the bad stuff to the good; about putting her faith in a God who endlessly forgives; about peeling away the layers of resentment and disappointment; about letting the light shine in all the darkness.

Bella went off to have a think about it.

The next day she was back. *I'll do it!*

Wonderful! When?

Tomorrow? After lunch?

The next day we got everything ready in the Crypt's lovely chapel. Water, in as beautiful a bowl as the kitchen staff could find us; oil, as a sign of blessing; a candle for her as a remembrance; Mark's gospel for her to keep; a clean white towel, and a copy of the words of the simple service, to take away, to reflect on, and find blessing.

We had everything ready for Bella's baptism. She didn't come. This has happened before; it can be a hopeful sign. A sign that our friends realize that this is a significant event: something that can change your life, if you let it. Joyful and solemn. It's a big ask. People get frightened.

We didn't see anything of Bella for a few days. Then she came back, slightly sheepishly. That's all right too; sheep get a good press in the gospels. I asked her, gently, if she still wanted to be baptised. She did: and said that here and now would be a good time.

We went through to chapel, and she helped me gather everything together; whatever else, the sacrament of baptism is a hallowing of the physical.

My Lighthouse colleague Jon Swales, who knows all his sheep, and knew Bella well, joined us; he hadn't been able to come on the last appointed day. Providence works.

We went through the service; I anointed Bella, and then Jon baptized her in the name of God who created her, of Jesus who lived and died for her, of the Spirit whose abiding presence has brought her to this moment.

Bella, I baptize you in the name of the Father, and of the Son, and of the Holy Spirit.

For a moment she stood absolutely still. Then she put her face in her hands and wept, and said, *Dear God, I wish I always felt this loved.*

There are moments when eternity breaks through; when the gracious love of God gently overwhelms us, and everything is put right. Afterwards, doubtless, it will seem different again. But there has been this moment. The light shines; and the darkness shall never, ever, overcome it.

HOW DO YOU READ ME?

G ot anything planned for the weekend, Father? Stan takes a genuine interest in what the rest of the world is doing. When you're on the streets, without work to give any rhythm to time, one day slides into another.

I'm going to look for a new sound system.

What sort do you want?

This is not an enquiry as to whether I've read the latest reviews. This is an offer to acquire me a sound system; and to specify the make and model. Stan has a string of convictions for burglary, and even more contacts. He could get you anything. I decline, with thanks; he means well, sort of. Pursing my lips and delivering a homily on the sanctity of material possessions isn't going to help. I just hold his gaze for a couple of seconds, trying not to laugh. Then he says, with the unexpectedness of many conversations in the Crypt,

Have you got any Bibles?

I presume this is a request, rather than an offer. Copies of the King James Version may fall off the back of a lorry, but their resale value is disappointingly low.

I am moved to reply, *How many do you want?* For all I know, he might be planning to set up a Bible study amongst the burglars of Leeds. Stranger things have happened at St George's Crypt.

He looks at me oddly, used to the weirdness of clergy. *Just the one'll do.*

I go off, and return with an attractive paperback of Luke's gospel, in an accessible translation. The whole Bible can be a bit much. Those who don't get lost in the smitings of Joshua and the evils of eating lobster can end up trying to read Revelation as though it were a horoscope. Apart from which, there's just

59

so much of it, especially if you're not a big reader. Not many of our people love nothing better than to bury themselves in the timeless classics of English literature. Giving them a book ten times longer than the average novel, written by eighty very diverse authors (at the last count), accurately but obscurely translated, is not always helpful. Often we need what one of our friends called a *parrot-phrase*.

The Simpsons is a programme of high moral tone masquerading as anarchy. In one episode Pastor Lovejoy is asked by Mo to recommend a passage which will answer to his needs. Like too many lazy clergy (may we be forgiven) he casually replies, *Oh, it's all good.*

The real difficulty is where people try to read the Scriptures as though they were a single book, written in one genre. That's like watching television for a whole day and not noticing the difference between news, documentary, drama, soaps and cartoons. The Bible deserves better. So do its readers.

THE KEY

Zeb is newly arrived at the Crypt. He's just got out of jail. Prison is tough at the best of times, but especially so now; with the threat of COVID, prisoners can be locked in their cells 23 hours a day. That's not good for anyone. Even monks don't spend that long banged up, and they are better resourced to cope with it, and have a choice (more or less). We are deeply thankful for those monastic communities who keep us in their prayers. Most of us find it hard to pray for half-an-hour. Archbishop Ramsey was asked how long he spent in prayer each day; his reply surprised his interviewer: *A couple of minutes.* Then he went on: *but it takes me an hour to get there.*

Zeb is from Holbeck, one of the less fashionable parts of the city I knew well as a child. He tells me he shot someone when he was drunk. I wonder whether this is better or worse than shooting someone when you're sober.

His little sister died; drugs. He finds faith a comfort. Often it's the crises that bring us to God; the birth of a child; the death of a loved one; marriage or divorce; these force us to consider what it's all about. Finding faith gives true perspective; gives meaning to the unbearable.

I suggest he visits the Lighthouse: he won't feel as out of place there as in a traditional church. He is worried about his

room, because it's not locked – he hasn't got a key yet. He will get one soon, on a very big key-ring, so he can't accidentally walk off with it. Being newly arrived, everything is strange, and so frightening. But that is often the place for healing: the true key.

JESU'S BLOOD

The men I remember from when I first volunteered at the Crypt in the late seventies were old-fashioned gentlemen of the road, otherwise called tramps. They would doff the flat cap which they all wore, and call you sir. One old Irishman told me that this might not always mean what it appeared to: *Sor* is the Irish Gaelic for a pig's louse.

Old Ted wanted to talk. We went through to chapel, and he shared his troubles. The courage of our people gets to me. The rest of us find it hard enough to cope with crisis; bereavement; losing a job; severe illness. Add to that being homeless; having nowhere to go home to, and no one who cares whether you live or die. Ted had tried to contact his daughter. She wanted nothing to do with him. And she was the last person left. He felt like he had come to the end of the road.

I'm useless. There'll be no one'll miss me when I'm gone.

We want to be remembered. We want to have made a difference. I couldn't find the words; whatever I thought to say would sound trite. When that happens, music can heal. I found a CD, and told him the story.

Around 1970, a documentary was made about people who were homeless in London. One man sang a song. It hadn't made it into the final cut; no one even knew his name. But the composer Gavin Bryars ended up with the tape. He put it on a loop, playing the 26 seconds of song over and over, in the open office he shared. When he came back from getting a coffee, the whole office had fallen silent; some were weeping. They knew nothing about it, but the singer, long dead, spoke to their hearts. Gavin took the song, and gently, sensitively, compassionately, weaved a growing accompaniment around the repeated song.

So I told Ted the story of *Jesu's Blood,* and played it for him. The song of a homeless man, otherwise quite forgotten, whose music lives on, touching the hearts of all who hear him.

We listened in silence. As tears coursed down his face, so they did down mine. In the heart of God, we are cherished forever. Our song is not forgotten.

THE HOPE OF LOVE

Vicky was troubled. So is everyone who comes to us. The Crypt is rock bottom, when there's nowhere else left. And I remember the courageous words of J. K. Rowling: *Rock Bottom became the solid foundation on which I rebuilt my life.* There is always hope. Vicky never lost hope. Not quite completely. We had talked. Everything had happened to her: abuse; abandonment; violence; unbearable disappointment; addiction to anything that might ease the pain for a little while, till the next time.

Then one day she looked a bit brighter. Her ex had texted and asked her to meet him in the small green space known to our people as *Pisshead Park* (hard by Hangover Square). It was a Thursday. Thursday was the day Vicky got her benefits, and her former lover knew it. She would have some money and he wanted it. They spent the day drinking, then arguing, then fighting. The next thing we knew Vicky was sitting, drunk and covered in blood, on the front wall by the Crypt. He had knocked her front tooth out. She sat there in shock, grieving for everything, again. *I used to be beautiful.*

For once she was persuaded by friends to bring charges against him. As I sat next to her, a police car arrived, and

we travelled together to A & E, near the Crypt. The policewoman was incredibly patient for the two hours it took Vicky to make a barely coherent Statement. I prayed that they would find room to keep her in for the night. The staff at the Infirmary were skilled and compassionate, and miraculously found space to give her a bed.

By the time I got back to the front door of the Crypt it was about eleven at night. A fight was breaking out. No big deal; it only needed me to tell one of them to go one way, and his friend the other; but somehow it had been picked up inside the Crypt, and half-a-dozen of our residents piled out to protect the chaplain. That was when it might have turned ugly. But the angels watch over us, and somehow everyone just drifted away. Then I heard a shout. *Roger!* Vicky had come out of the back door of the hospital, grasping her shirt: *I can't stay like this; I'm covered in bloody blood!* Somehow she'd noticed. I asked what room she was staying in, and went off to find her a cleaner t-shirt. By the time I got back out, she had hooked up with one of the men outside, and gone off again, in the forlorn but everlasting hope of love. Or just a few moments of fleeting affection.

Whatever happened then, by the early hours the hospital ward had let her back in. The next day she was back with us. At lunchtime she came up to me, and gave me a kiss on the cheek, like a little child. *For of such is the kingdom of heaven.*

Over the next year or so, we saw Vicky fairly regularly. She got pregnant, and then took up with another of our regulars. (His story, *Letting Go*, is told in *Entertaining Saints*.) She went into labour very early; the little girl was born premature, and her life hung in the balance. I promised Vicky I would go up to the neo-natal unit, and pray for her child. After we had talked a little, the nurse told me that the mother wasn't coming to see her baby. She didn't understand why. Hospital staff don't have enough time; she couldn't have read all of Vicky's voluminous notes.

As gently as I could, I explained that the mother already had eight children; all in care. She knew that this child too would be taken from her. She didn't want to get close to her. That would only make their parting harder.

65

Vicky was glad to know I had been. The little child thrived enough to go to one of the wonderful foster-mothers who care for babies with such particular needs; who may be born addicted, and have to go through withdrawal, and may be HIV positive at birth. Their care and devotion, and skill, is beyond expressing; not least in that they too know they must bond with a child, and then give them up to an uncertain future.

Vicky's partner, himself an addict, died within the year. A short time after, we heard that she too had died, still in her thirties. We miss her.

BY THE LAKE

Kevin had been with us nearly two years at Faith Lodge. Our old dry house ran a strict regime, and he had stayed clean of the drugs which had nearly destroyed him. Then one day – for whatever reason we never fully discovered – he went off with another resident to score. He used the same amount of heroin he always had. But his body wasn't used to it anymore, and in the morning his poor friend found Kevin dead on the floor. That's where he was when I saw him the next morning, awaiting the arrival of the coroner's officials. I stood over his body, and prayed for him, that God our most loving father would heal all his hurt, and take him to himself, and let him, somehow, be all that he was created to be.

Everyone was shocked by his death. He was only a lad; still in his twenties. We loved him. But it wasn't enough.

We needed to do something. So we took all the residents out for lunch in a good pub, sharing our memories, our laughter and our tears. Then we went together for a walk around Roundhay Park Lake, because life goes on. Walking together after death. Like the road to Emmaus. But there was no moment of revelation here. Only grief. And the hope against hope that there could be something beyond this life. The dead body I had seen was not him. Only the shell. But the risen Lord appears to us on the shore of the lake, and gives us his peace. *Lord, quickly come.*

AND ON MY
BIRTHDAY

We try to protect our people. Sometimes the hardest part of this is protecting them from each other. Denis was spectacularly camp, and usually preferred to be called *Denise*. Occasionally he would turn up in a light summer frock, and flounce around, shrieking with laughter and fluttering his false eyelashes. Most people saw all this as a bit of fun; our people are often more accepting than the rest of the world. On the rare occasions when someone did pass some slighting comment, Denise defended himself with cheerful courage and a razor-sharp wit.

Just occasionally, it would get a bit much. We discovered that he had been not only propositioning the younger men, but allegedly encouraging them into prostitution. We don't ban people completely; there always has to be space for repentance. But this time it fell to me to put him on *Restriction*. A couple of weeks without access to the Crypt seemed appropriate.

He was outraged.

Well! I think it's disgusting. Taking my rights away. And on my birthday as well.

We had been here before.

Denise, you've had three birthdays already this year.

He was not to be put off.

Well it's my mother's birthday then.

It was your mother's birthday two months ago. Or so you told us anyhow.

Well. It might have been. But she wasn't very old.

His lower lip began to tremble. With all the sorrow in his life, tears were always accessible.

Never mind. It's only a couple of weeks. When you come back you can have another birthday.

He brightened considerably. *Can I have a cake as well?*

Don't push it. Maybe.

And so he went off, almost happily. We aim to please.

DOMESTIC STREET

Our old wet house on Regent Terrace in Hyde Park had got too old and tired. The floor was going through in places, the roof leaked, the bathrooms were a mess, the kitchens were past it. We did what we could to care for the fifteen alcoholic men who otherwise would have been on the streets. For years, like the older lads who lived there, we'd been doing our best. Then it came to the crunch. We couldn't patch things up anymore. It needed a new build.

Somehow, miraculously, the money came. Enough for a complete new building. Not just that, but instead of single rooms we could provide everyone with their own flat. Somewhere to call their own. But what to do in the meantime? Our people had known enough disruption and uncertainty in their lives. We wanted to stay together; to still be a family.

Then somewhere came up. In Holbeck, on Domestic Street. The council owned a big old house which when it was built a hundred years before must have been rather splendid. There were still traces of that now, in its high ceilings and ornate fireplaces. Apart from that, it had been left derelict, taken over by drug users. We filled two large bins with used tackle: needles and condoms. We didn't have long. Our indefatigable centre manager spent every hour of every day working to bring it up to standard. But it still wasn't going to be ready in time. We would have to close down part of the Crypt whilst every member of staff joined in everything that needed doing. And it still wouldn't be ready. Then Chris got a phone call out of the blue. *This is Leeds College of Building. Could you use a team of plasterers and decorators for anything? We've got a spare week.* I don't even remember us praying for that. But sometimes in prayer, unable to see a way out, you just throw the whole thing up to God and pray *You sort it out.*

A couple of days before we were due to move the lads in to their new temporary home, I went round the now wonderfully restored building, and prayed God's blessing on it all. Then I noticed the carpet warehouse next door. It hadn't always sold carpets. Isle Lane Chapel had been a flourishing Wesleyan church back in the day. Some of my family had loved it dearly a century ago. And so, as I left, I lifted my eyes and asked them; the faithful of generations long gone, to keep an eye on our people. To pray for them and keep them safe. Methodist doctrine doesn't usually include prayer to the saints, but I hoped they would forgive me. Sometimes there is a sense of prayer being heard.

The lads stayed there for a year while their new home was rising like a phoenix from the ashes of the old. It was a good home for them, until the new one was ready. That's how it always is in the end. *For here we have no abiding city.*

MANCHESTER BOB AND THE SPIDER

Manchester Bob was one of the old sort. What they used to call a gentleman of the road. Sober, he was a delight, with a dry sense of humour and a real kindness. After a few drinks he was appalling, violent and dangerous. He came regularly to church on a Sunday morning; maybe believing, maybe hopeful; much like the rest of us. Maybe knowing that he might get a few cigs and a bit of money if he was lucky. We all hope for reward one way or another; spiritually or socially. The motives of the faithful are never straightforward.

One Sunday over coffee we were chatting when I watched a spider drop down from his ragged beard. It came down a few inches, then crawled back up into its hairy home. I considered mentioning it, then thought that it would only embarrass him, and possibly the spider. Neither of them seemed in the least troubled.

Our expectations are different; Churches are clean and respectable for the most part. But if the prophet Elijah was fed by ravens, and John the Baptist ate locusts, we need to think again. According to legend, Robert the Bruce was taught fortitude by a spider; in the biblical account, David was saved by a spider's web. I overcame a fear of spiders by getting to know them better. These days I rescue them from my house, and release them into the wild. But there they will prey on other insects, so that my act of apparent charity also makes me an accessory to murder; or at least insecticide. The moral web, the consideration of motive, can leave us spinning in circles; but there is a value in spontaneity. We trust.

HISTORIES

We prayed this morning for peace in America, by talking about it. Our conversations range widely, and because those conversations happen in the middle of our service, they are hallowed; given to God. Normally this happens in response to our Bible reading. We each bring our several histories, our different lives, our joys and sorrows, and share them. I talk too much. Most Christians – and all clergy – talk too much. In prayer we ask God for a whole list of things, and don't wait for a reply.

Listening gives us insight, new perspectives. My friend John Mackendrick wrote:

> … *it's about catching an angle of God's face that no one's ever seen before. Give it blood!*

So as I listen to Gareth talking about Fountains Abbey, I see it – one of my favourite places in all the world – in a different way. He tells us that his time in Bosnia, seeing bombed-out buildings, taught him to see the Cistercian ruins in a new light; that it once was a place destroyed, torched, attacked, *slighted*. I will never again see that beautiful and tranquil place in quite the same way. It has become something else, something more; closer maybe to God's perception of it, who knows all our yesterdays.

And so we talked of perspective, and of the need to understand those who stormed the Capitol two days ago. Those who have – whatever else – felt unrepresented, disenfranchised, patronised by the powerful and remote. It is not congenial to put your mind into such a place.

Cromwell, in a letter to the Scots Kirk, says:

I beseech you, in the bowels of Christ, think it possible you may be mistaken.

It is little comfort to think that they might as easily have put the same request to him.

Something like an answer comes from considering again that question we must ask when faced with any belief different from our own: *Why do they need to believe what they do?* There is always some sort of inner logic, however twisted.

As always, the question we ask as we conclude our prayer time together is, *How does all that affect what we do today?* How will this change our lives? Maybe it will encourage us to listen with compassion to those who come to us for help; who have their own histories, which have shaped their minds. *Lord, teach us how to pray.*

WHIRLPOOL

Benny's story is complex. It involves the death of many people; his partner's addiction, assault and miscarriage; his family's rejection; spells in prison; threats of violence and murder. I can't quite follow it all. A recurrent theme was a long saga involving a bed being moved. I wonder at the significance of this. It is all very dark; there is a spirit of loss and desolation; of brokenness and despair and fear. I do not know what to say. I don't know what he is asking of us. I don't think he knows himself. It is an inarticulate howling. *Out of the depths.*

Some of this at least is the result of whatever wicked substance he is off and on at the moment. Then his phone rings. He tells me it is his girlfriend. I bless him with the sign of the cross, and tell him we can talk again later. He nods distractedly, and takes a quick drag on the rollup he hasn't noticed isn't lit.

His confusion and anger and grief and despair swirl and roar. My little boat is on the edge of his whirlpool, but needs to come close enough to offer a lifeline. All I can do for the moment is to tell my colleagues, and give it to God, who alone can still the waves.

Sometimes it is hard to know where to start. But that's not true. We always start from *here*. It's not knowing the direction of travel that makes it hard to move at all. But the way of faith is like coming to the end of everything you have known and loved, then being asked to step off into the darkness, trusting that there will be loving arms to catch you; or you will be taught how to fly.

THE HOUSE OF FUN

Morning Prayer today had one of the cheerier bits of Ecclesiastes:

Sorrow is better than laughter: for by the sadness of the countenance the heart is made better. The heart of the wise is in the house of mourning; but the heart of fools is in the house of mirth.

Well, yes. Or rather *No*. As it happens, I attended a Jewish funeral yesterday. What stayed with me was not necessarily the prayers and readings – beautiful and surely comforting though those are. Rather I was struck by how the grave was being filled by the mourners, who each put in three small amounts of earth using the back of the spade. This was explained to me: by doing this *we acknowledge that it has to be done, but also express our unwillingness to do it.* It expresses both the inevitability and the intense pain of loss.

Pondering those things, I had a conversation with one of our lads, now months into recovery from addiction, sharing a house with others going through the same process. He told me about his weekend; how they had sat down for a meal together, and how wonderful it was that they could share laughter together without needing some narcotic substance to get them there. It was like he'd remembered how to laugh again. Certainly his face has changed over the many months I've known him; a weight of fear and darkness has fallen away. Mostly. All that still flickers sometimes. But the shared laughter helps.

So, what about Ecclesiastes? Well, my mind goes back to Julian of Norwich, whose most-quoted line loses by not including the first three words, which somehow make sense of a whole lot more: *Sin is necessary. But all shall be well, and all shall be well, and all manner of things shall be well.*

JUDGEMENT

A lbert was in a very dark place last week. Coming off drugs for the first time in years, he dropped into a state of depression. Happily, he talked about it, and together we were able to encourage him. Now he is in a very different place. He tells me that he used to play football, and should have been a professional, but never made it. I guess the drugs had robbed him of all that might have been. He qualified as a referee, and wasn't afraid to take tough decisions and stand by them. That's not easy: judgement never is. We pray often for the work of the courts just round the corner from the Crypt. This morning in prayers we read the story of the woman found guilty of adultery, and about judging and not judging. Compassion; putting yourself in the other person's place. When you say that God is love, some people will quickly tell you that God is justice as well. They often seem to value the judge more than the lover. But God's justice is not about retribution; it is about putting all to rights.

Asked to judge the case of the woman taken in adultery, why did Jesus write on the ground? Maybe to show that the law is provisional; it gets blown away when the wind of the Spirit blows. *The letter kills; but the Spirit gives life.*

TOGETHER

Jamie asks me to talk to Matt. We trust one another, offering what help we can; practically, spiritually, mentally. Some of my colleagues know the benefits system inside out; some know how soiled bedding needs to be washed; others know about addiction; our chefs know how to provide nourishing meals from whatever is kindly donated; our fundraising staff keep us solvent; our managers hold it all together, by the God-given miracles which have preserved St George's Crypt for over ninety years.

Matt has just heard that his ex has died. In fact she died weeks ago, but no one told him. He found out on Facebook. We go into our chapel together. It is being used as a storeroom during lockdown, but my colleagues kindly agree to go somewhere else while I talk to Matt. That gives us ten minutes to talk through death, grief, hope and forgiveness. All of which we do, and pray for Coral, his ex, that all her hurt be healed. He shows me a picture of them in happier times; they made a handsome couple. Then drugs robbed them of all that. You think you can cope. Just using one more time won't hurt. You've got it under control. Next thing, you've lost everything. Coral had spent time in prison. What killed her? Probably overdose; he doesn't know. Something prompts me to ask Matt where he's from. The Gipton. I used to live there too, when it was the white sink estate for Leeds. We remember the faithful priests who served there.

Our ten minutes is up. He is talking, and finding support, from others as well; that's the important thing. Not to go into himself, not to *go off on one*. We will hold him together in a gentle embrace until the storm has passed; which it will.

STANDARDS

Harold has been one of our regulars for many years, and looks like it. He knows how to survive, and wears the sort of waxy jacket designed to keep you warm and dry while shooting or fly fishing, neither of which he is likely to do on the streets of Leeds. All sorts of legends have gathered around him. It's said that he might once have been a lawyer, or an accountant; he loves music, and has a particular liking for Joni Mitchell. Commendable. Certainly, like his coat, he has seen better days. He has a fondness for York; not simply to enjoy the historic delights of that ancient city, but rather because the well-heeled tourists tend to be generous. One Christmas he told me he'd made £387 in a single day. Begging can be lucrative, especially if you look unwashed and desperately in need, which he generally, and perhaps deliberately, does. After a few drinks, he spits when talking.

At one point he was living in our Wet House; the old building on Regent Terrace. In the middle of the student area of Hyde Park, our rather dilapidated house – perhaps surprisingly – was one of the quieter ones. He seemed to be getting on all right. Then one of the staff noticed that he was only eating half his meals, and slipping the rest into one of his voluminous pockets. This led to his being watched a bit more closely, which eventually revealed that he had installed a friend into one of the outhouses. She too had her problems, and Harold was not the least of them. As one of his fellow residents put it, *He's been keeping a mucky woman in the garage.*

She, poor soul, had been granting her favours in return for food and drink. And perhaps a bit of affection. Other people's relationships are often hard to assess.

Under the circumstances (of which this was only the culmination) we asked him – and his friend – to leave. Offered alternative accommodation in the Crypt itself, he was not keen to take up the offer. *I've got standards you know.*

We all, I suppose, have *standards*. Different ways we define ourselves. Harold's just happen to be a bit different from most.

JUSTICE

B ill was one of the first homeless people I got to know well. Originally from Glasgow, he had been a marine engineer before booze took its toll. We saw him slide down from near-respectability to down-and-out, sleeping rough. One morning he was in unusually good spirits, and called me over enthusiastically:

Here! I've a story to tell you. When sober, he was quite the raconteur.

I got taken in last night by the police. Nothing unusual there; after a few drinks he tended to break shop windows. Whether this was deliberate, accidental, or just out of general frustration with the world was often not clear, either to the courts, or us – or probably to him.

So this morning I get put up in front of the judge and he says to me, "Mr Dawson, why were you begging in the public highway?"

This is an ancient offence, sometimes used by the police to apprehend a miscreant before worse happens.

So I says tae him, I says, "Because, Your Honour, I would rather beg than steal!"

Bill looks uncommonly pleased with himself.

And he says tae me, "That seems a very fair point. Case Dismissed!" What do you think eh, what do you think!?

He is by now almost dancing for joy. I don't blame him. It is not often that one of our guys so successfully makes his own defence in court.

A few months later, sleeping rough and inevitably drunk on Woodhouse Moor, some youths thought it fun to set light to him. His hand and face were badly burned and permanently scarred. Within a short time, he just disappeared, and we never saw him again. This all happened years ago. Bill will be long gone, to where he may hope for even better justice than is found in this earthly court.

NOT YOUR BUSINESS

Sometimes we just get a feeling about people. A sense of unhappiness, or imbalance, or threat. This isn't to do with any particular gift of extra-sensory perception, or even spiritual discernment – though I believe all sensitivity comes from God. What matters, as with any gift, is how you use it. Gabriel volunteers on our signing-in desk at lunchtime (archangels are useful), and has an extraordinary gift of memory for names and faces. I have only to ask him, this day, for the name of one of our guests, and he knows immediately. He too picked up something to be wary of; a tall, bearded man, by his name probably from Eastern Europe.

I stroll around the lunch tables, keeping half an eye on our friend, and praying. Praying for those around him, and for him also, that whatever is troubling him might be resolved. Something upsets him, and he shouts angrily; apparently to himself rather than anyone else. We watch carefully, in case this develops into something else. It doesn't, but there is a sense of a coiled spring about him. I go back to the desk, hoping to catch him on his way out, at a point where he doesn't have to engage if he doesn't want to; hoping to help, maybe. He pushes through the door and pauses for a moment. I take my chance.

How are you today my friend?

He turns away from me and stares up at the ceiling. When he turns back his face is angry, contorted.

Is not your business!

And with that he strides away. Gabriel and I look at each other, slightly shocked, then laugh out loud. It's not often that a gentle enquiry meets such a fierce response. The laughter is important. Freud said that laughter is a release of psychic tension. Commenting on that, the wonderful Ken Dodd – who surely knew more about laughter than anyone – said: *Freud never had to play third house on a Saturday at the Glasgow Empire.* Nor, to my knowledge, did the father of psychoanalysis spend much time in a homeless shelter. We take what experience we are given, and pray to make good use of it. For a moment, I had felt frightened; maybe in the face of spiritual malaise, poor man. To which the only and best response is love offered freely, offered as prayer.

Even if I don't remember his name now; Gabriel will. The angels surround us.

BIKER

Tony lived in our old house on Regent Terrace. He did his best to look like the biker he once had been; his hair long, worn in a way that might have been fashionable and attractive forty years before. It was less so now; thinned and greasy. He didn't seem to notice. He walked still with a slight swagger, as though strolling up to the bar in a Western saloon. We would go outside for a smoke, and talk about motorbikes we had owned a long time ago. A sudden flash of light would come into his eyes as he re-lived cornering fast and scraping the foot-pegs of his machine. Something about him reminded me of the leader of a biker gang I had known in Holland; a tall man, bearded, with eyes that had seen too much. He came up to me, prodded my clerical collar and said *You priest?* I weighed up the chances; then stroked his beard and said, *You prophet?* It could have gone either way. For a long moment there was silence. Then he roared with laughter, threw his massive arm around my shoulders and shouted *Beer!* We had a good night.

Similarly vivid memories haunted Tony; some good, some bad. Like so many of our friends he did not want to remember his childhood, but couldn't let it go. He felt a failure as a husband and father; his family wanted nothing to do with him. Then, quite suddenly, he died. I missed our conversations, and I miss his very distinct presence. I miss not having got to know him better, not having used better the time allotted.

MEMORIES

In the lunch queue today, I find myself behind Betty. She came to Leeds from a Glasgow tenement many years ago. We've talked often enough of Scotland, where she knows I spent some time. Finding common ground is important. Suddenly she turns to me:

Do you miss Scotland?

From our previous conversations, I can understand that her move to Yorkshire has not been all she might have hoped for; it brought her to the Crypt, after all.

Aye Betty, I do miss Scotland.

Well I don't. It's pish.

Trying not to laugh, I reflect that the notorious area where she grew up might not have been so kind to her as my own experience in rural Perthshire.

Is Leeds better then? This is itself a dangerous question, but one that might just call to her mind what might be better than the life she left.

Oh aye. I've friends here now.

And that makes all the difference. For any of us, being alone, isolated, friendless, is the worst thing. Relationships can be bad –

 appalling even – but too often it feels like anything is better than nothing. It isn't. Domestic abuse destroys lives. Moving away is always risky; the biggest danger is that no matter what you manage to escape, you've still got yourself to cope with. And when that self has dark memories, leaving them behind can be hard indeed. But it's possible. Life can be better than ever you dared hope. Betty is living proof.

REMEMBRANCE

Remembrance is a significant time in the Crypt. Many of our people are haunted by memories, and all have known friends who died too young. We name those who have died in the year just gone, and commend them to the loving mercy of God. In an average year, more than twenty of our friends die. We keep the two minutes silence, and end with the traditional words: *They shall not grow old as we that are left grow old.* Too many of them never had the chance to grow old. It is said that the average age of death if you are homeless is about 45: even less for women, who are more vulnerable. We see many die much younger; in their twenties, their lives barely begun. And we rage against the dying of the light, knowing how much they had to gain; to learn; to live. And it is no good saying that God wanted them. We wanted them.

Acting as padre to the Cameronians, I visited with them the Reichswald cemetery in Germany. By tradition, we were each given crosses to place on individual graves, as we felt moved. One soldier, at 27, was older than most. His headstone gave his name, rank and regiment. The family was allowed to choose whatever they wished to be inscribed at the base; frequently a verse of Scripture. Not so in his case; it simply said, *My dear daddy.*

I found it difficult to get through the drum-head ceremony which followed.

Our people become statistics easily. Their lives are not valued, their deaths barely mourned.

All we can do is to entrust them to the love of God, and make their best memorial our care for those who are still with us; at the going down of the sun, and in the morning.

TAPESTRY

We try to make sense of things. Our lives go on, more or less smoothly, and then suddenly some disaster changes everything. A line has been drawn, and we find ourselves saying, *Before the accident* or *Before he got cancer* or *Before she died*. Our people come to us weighed down with disasters of which homelessness is only the most recent. Like any of us, they want to make sense of their experience. We look back, and try to find meaning in it all. Sometimes this is possible. I have heard more than one person say, *Losing that job was the best thing that ever happened. Didn't feel like it at the time.* It never does. Other things – murder, the suffering of a child – these are immeasurably, unbearably harder to comprehend.

I remembered the story of a tapestry. I had never seen it, but heard that it looked a complete mess; a confused bundle of threads. I told this to our good friend Catherine, who faithfully runs the arts and crafts group in the Crypt after lunch on Fridays. A few weeks later she gave me – unasked – the tapestry our people had made. It was a riotous mess of colour, threads hanging loose, with no discernible pattern. Then she turned it round.

The other side was beautifully and neatly worked; the point of it all became evident. At its centre is a shining golden cross.

For those of us who can believe, it is so. This life alone makes no sense; there are only moments, hints of meaning. Only from the other side can we understand as we are understood. Even that sounds too facile. But when Jesus comes back from death to his friends, he still bears the scars. Even the cross becomes gold.

NUDGE

Listening to God can be tricky. All sorts of people have thought they knew what God was wanting them to do. According to the Bible those things have included genocide, war, violent racism, and just about anything else. My own experience has been more gentle, thank God, though I am wary. Sometimes, walking down a corridor in the Crypt, I have felt what feels like a nudge to go into a particular room. No big deal. Certainly no light from on high. Just a hint of a suggestion; *just drop in there*. And sometimes, though not always, I follow the nudging. So sometimes I find myself having gone into an office and see my dear colleagues all looking at me. Did I want something? And sometimes the best answer I can give is, *I just came to give you all a blessing*. Sometimes that's where it ends. Apparently; but who knows what comes of a blessing? Or sometimes there is a reply: *Thank God, I need to talk*.

We do what we can. The work of the Crypt is often deeply demanding, more costly than we can always acknowledge. Then we need to turn again; to pray if we can; to take comfort in the constant abiding presence of God's Holy Spirit. That's one way of putting it. On a human level, we are encouraged by knowing that we're not in this alone. That we work together as a team; that it's not all about me. That's good. But if you believe in something more, the good expands to infinity, and the gentle nudge in the corridor becomes part of the pattern of eternity; a blessing; a conversation. Another beautiful stitch in the fabric of the universe.

CURRENT CONCERNS

Most people leave the Crypt for somewhere better; the Council houses them, or they get a place in one of our Growing Rooms. We calculate about 85 per cent have what can be called a *positive move on*. I am never sure whether going to prison counts as a positive move or not. At least people are warm, and fed and housed. A lot depends on the sort of offence they've committed, and where they serve their time. During a pandemic, anywhere is bad.

One of the lads, living in one of our houses, came in to volunteer at the Crypt. We are grateful for their help; and it gives their lives some purpose. But Sid was unhappy. Recently released from prison, he was wearing an electronic tag. The conditions of being tagged are very strict. Sid was beside himself because he suddenly remembered he'd forgotten to charge his tag. If it stopped sending the necessary signal back, showing that he was where he was supposed to be at the right time, he would get recalled to prison immediately; no excuses accepted. Christine drove up to his house, and brought his charger back for him. He was hugely relieved, and effusively grateful.

The next problem only emerged a little while later, when we found him plugged into the mains and vigorously mopping the floor. He readily accepted our advice that electricity and water don't mix, and that he was in danger of blowing himself and possibly the rest of us somewhere even closer to heaven than the Crypt. He took the point, and readily accepted more static (and drier) duties.

Thankfully, the judicial system in this country does not include fatal electrocution. If it had done in Jesus' time, we would all be wearing little gold electric chairs on necklaces.

LAFAYETTE, NOUS VOILÀ

This morning we have some visitors. An American delegation is visiting St George's Church; they are interested to know more of our work in the Crypt. They join us for Morning Prayer in our beautiful chapel, where we sit surrounded by paintings of former clients, taking their place as the disciples gathered with Jesus at their last meal together. I suspect that our visitors' tradition would not regularly include the set form of liturgy we use. They receive it nonetheless graciously, generously, and afterwards we move into a time of open prayer together. We surround one another with prayer, and find ourselves caught up in a time of blessing, in which many of us are moved to tears. We pray together, gently and quietly, for all those who come through our doors looking for help. We pray for my colleagues, that we may be given grace not only to minister, but to recognize as our brothers and sisters in Christ all who come to us.

It becomes a time of extraordinary grace and blessing, and I confess to God my wariness of their visit. Maybe it's just being English – or more probably, being half-Canadian – that makes me suspicious of brash American religion, may I be forgiven. But that morning there was no doubting the presence of the Holy Spirit as we prayed together, and shared the incidental diversity, and infinite unity, of compassion; of love, of faith.

KEEP WALKING

I mention Mirfield, where I trained for the priesthood. Jason tells me he grew up in Mirfield; he tells me about his early life there in a children's home. We share another experience, of taking our baby sons to the same local hospital. Mine lived, his died. My son is grown-up now, making his own way in the world. And his son? I believe that no life is lost to God; that every one of us will become, in His love, everything we were created to be. That includes those who die in the womb, like my friend's son. Jesus says: *I have not lost one of those you gave me.*

A few days later, Jason asks me for a rosary; he wants it to hang around the picture of his little son. I give him the one I always have in my pocket, and we pray, that it may be a sign of God's love surrounding us, in this life and in the next.

Afterwards, he tells me that the prayer gave him goose-bumps. I tell him this can be a sign of healing; of being in touch once again with real feeling. Not pretend feelings; not feelings distorted, twisted or numbed by drugs or booze; *real* feelings which are a mixture of joy and pain, which live close together in the human soul. We don't need to feel that. It's just another blessing, which God seems to give often – but not only – to those beginning another part of the pilgrimage. We receive it gladly, and keep walking.

In the Way

One of our residents had to be restrained yesterday. He was running up and down one of the busiest dual carriageways in Leeds, where he was a danger to traffic and to himself. When questioned, he tells us that he is a car, travelling at a hundred miles an hour. We point out that he is a human being, and that other road users have been honking at him. He patiently explains to us that they were honking to encourage him, impressed that he was going so fast. He had been driven to do this (see what I did there?) by a combination of already serious mental health problems, and whatever narcotic garbage he had got hold of this time.

His story followed on from this morning's gospel reading, where Andrew brings Greeks to Jesus, which leads to a vision of glory. Quite why, I am not sure; just as I am not sure how this connects with our motorised friend. We try to connect our readings with our daily life; otherwise, what's the point? Maybe by the end of today I might have figured it out. Or maybe my explanation will make as much sense as believing the other drivers are honking encouragement. We see through a glass, darkly. Sometimes the meaning will have to wait till we see face to face. Which in our friend's case – happily and miraculously – was not yesterday.

CHANGING THE TIME

I am sitting quietly at my desk when suddenly the room explodes. *Where's the ladders?* Baz doesn't do quiet. I am touched that he thinks I might be organised enough to know where we keep ladders. The clocks went forward this week, and he wants to change the clock in our Assisi Café, where we are holding Morning Prayer during lockdown. This would be helpful; I struggle to keep to the fifteen minutes we are allowed together during the pandemic. He finds a ladder and changes the clock. I ask if anyone needs prayer this morning. Baz tells us that Joe's sister has died; after months of being clean of drugs he has started using again. We pray for him, and for his sister.

It is Holy Week, and talk of death is never far from our thoughts. It was only last year that Joe was able – after many years of estrangement – to finally make contact with his family again. It's not always easy to maintain a good relationship with family. For our people that difficulty is magnified by lives which have distanced them; if they had been able to go to loving families, they would not have come to the Crypt. They come to us dragging behind them a rattling hinterland of broken and damaged relationships. Then too much time has passed for them to know what to say when they make that phone call. News somehow gets through that one of the family has died, and grief is added to the unbearable guilt and regret; it's too late now.

And yet in God's eternity it's never too late. *Be not faithless but believing.* But you have to share the pain; to feel the wounds. No hiding.

Time is not straightforward; we lose and gain hours carelessly. But it's never, ever, too late.

INTERRUPTION

Jeff puts his head round my door, just to say good morning. The paper I am reading about homelessness, from an all-parliamentary group (fascinating though it is) can wait. It was working in a hospice that taught me to seize the moment; there will not be another chance for this conversation. Given that this morning has brought news of the death of another of our friends, this may be literally true. I remember Bonhoeffer:

We must be ready to allow ourselves to be interrupted by God.

Jeff tells me about his journey here today. He walked the couple of miles in from Armley, where he shares a house with three other recovering addicts. He has not gone far when one of his old friends, still in addiction, crosses the street to meet him. He says he is about to use the drugs he has just scored. Does Jeff want to go with him? Just once more for old times' sake? Jeff looks frightened and angry as he tells me; frightened at the constant pull of the old life; angry that it still has the power to seduce and call him back into the shadows. Almost. Somehow he found the strength to say no. He described his friend's sickly smile before he walked away. Our eyes meet. I know the look he had been given; from

 those in addiction who hold onto the shreds of their self-respect by appearing to pity the rest of us. Jeff is part of a new community now. He found the strength he needed today. Pray God he finds it tomorrow.

NAMES

Dog has decided he doesn't want to be Dog any more. He has been Dog for as long as we've known him, which is some years. But now, after years of struggle, he is moving into a new place; spiritually and physically. He can't quite believe it himself, and is wary. Too many memories of too many failures. So now he is Jack, which is the name he grew up with. Dog was his street name. The changing of names is important. It was important for Jacob, for Simon, and for Saul. Some people still take a new name at baptism; on converting to Judaism; or reverting to Islam.

Change isn't safe. One of the very hardest things for an addict (and we are all addicted to something) is turning your back on the group you were part of; the group that somehow – however twistedly – defined who you were, who knew you by name. It happens everywhere. Those who earn obscene amounts of money in the City refer to the rest of us as *civilians*. Churches are not immune to this clubableness; but as Archbishop Temple said, *The Church exists primarily for the sake of those who are still outside it.*

Names are important in the Scriptures because your name expressed the essence of who you were. The Hebrew name of God, transliterated as YHWH, may stand for a name of infinite length; one which literally cannot be pronounced. That is naming the glory; Wesley translates the infinite: *Whose nature and whose name is Love.*

WRESTLING JACOB

I srael is the only country on Earth named in honour of a wrestler. Struggling with the nature of belief is deep in the psyche of his descendants.

I asked a Jewish friend why all my Jewish friends would only ever answer one question with another. His reply delighted me: *Questions? What questions?*

One of our friends is struggling this morning. It is the anniversary of his wife's death, for which he blames himself. We often do, one way or another. Visiting bereaved families, I would almost always hear one of them say, *I was going to go and see her on Tuesday.* As if, somehow, that visit could have changed the course of everything; she might not have died. We want to control that which in the end cannot be controlled.

It is hard to believe that everything works together for good. It sounds like an easy get-out. In the face of the great tragedies of the world it can feel close to blasphemy. How can the suffering of innocents, hatred, holocaust, all possibly work together for good? If you want an easy answer you've asked the wrong question. But we don't have to resolve it all at once. At any one point, we can say *It's God's will.* We can say that immediately, with something close to fatalism; or we can wrestle with it until we have no strength left, and have just hammered out one more doctrine of theodicy. It all depends on how big a space you want for the mystery to resonate. In the end, either way, is infinite mystery.

When Jacob wrestled with God, he saw the angels *ascending and descending.* The rabbis ask why that way round; surely the angels should be descending from heaven, then ascending back up? They return the answer: the angels have always been with us; we just didn't notice.

RESEARCH

Organizations take on a life of their own. The easiest path is to continue doing the same thing, reacting to external needs, and changing only in response to them, if at all. Daily prayer together in the Crypt reminds us that we live and work in the context of eternity. We are blessed to be doing something whose bottom line is love, not money. This can intrigue the rest of the world, whose values are often different. So we welcome research; it provides something like an objective appraisal, and requires us to reflect.

Our longest research project is still running; funded by the Halley Stewart foundation, whose object is *to enable human flourishing and to prevent suffering.* We began by considering what difference – if any – being a faith-based organisation made to our delivery of service. We hoped that it might; we believe it does, immeasurably. Then COVID arrived, and our focus became if not different, then at least more specific. Research, at its best, is about listening, and looking. Working out what questions to ask is important, and often difficult.

If Churches worked better, they would be laboratories of the spirit, where we could truly explore. Too often we are given answers to questions we haven't asked. According to the gospels, Jesus asks a lot more questions than he answers. If we are to follow his example, don't we need to do the same?

THE CLEANING DANCE

The Crypt needs a lot of cleaning. Those who come to us for help are often in a state of confusion; keeping things clean and tidy is not their first priority. Our staff cleaners do the dirtiest of jobs with grace, courage, and unfailing good humour. We rely too on volunteers; especially those who are part of our Growing Rooms project, where men in recovery from addiction live in houses shared with three others and take part in a full-time programme which gives them hope, and the possibility of change. They volunteer to help keep the Crypt clean, and help in the kitchens. Often they start this slightly unwillingly, and I don't blame them. But somehow, in this act of service to others, freely given, they find a deeper purpose. I greet one of them as he begins to clean our Assisi Café. He doesn't hear me at first, then I notice his earbuds, and realize he's listening to music. He apologizes, then explains that the music helps him work: *It turns cleaning into dancing.* This may put a different gloss on what one of our friends told me, that *Muslims get called to prayer from the minuet.*

Even cleaning the floor can become something more – as George Herbert says,

> *Who sweeps a room as for thy laws*
> *Makes that and th'action fine.*

LIFT THINE EYES

Nicki had been sold into prostitution when she was six years old. By her mother. We knew her mother also, whose life had not been much better. As one of our friends put it, *the penny doesn't drop far from the tree*. Probably her grandmother had come to the Crypt as well. It's enough to make you believe in original sin. But we believe in hope. Getting our people to believe that is sometimes more difficult. After one especially sad conversation with Nicki, I tried to encourage her by asking,

If you could have anything – anything in the whole world – what would it be?

There was a moment of cloudy thought. Then her face brightened:

Ooh! A flat in Moortown.

Moortown is on the posher north side of Leeds; even there, there is some council housing, which is admittedly more *desirable* (as the estate agents say) than other neglected parts of the city.

That's the problem when you've been ground down by life, all of your life. Your perspective gets limited to the very close

at hand; your horizon is right in front of you. The question was meant to let her imagination fly; just for a moment to dream of something wildly, crazily lovely.

Nicki could have had anything in her imagination, but even her dreams were confined to what might just be possible. She'd had all the dreams knocked out of her long ago.

WALKING IT OFF

Our guys do a lot of walking. Buses are expensive in Leeds. If you need to visit Housing Options, the York Street medical centre, the chemist and the Job Centre, that's a round trip of about five miles on foot. Add to that the sort of dismal rain that Yorkshire specialises in, feet already sore from too much walking in worn-out trainers, and a state of health damaged by neglect and sleeping rough, it's like climbing a mountain.

One of the many challenges of being homeless is simply boredom. Life has become purposeless. Some people take to walking around the city, which can give the illusion of intent – to the walker, and to anyone who sees them. Alec was a troubled young man, not yet thirty, whose background was complicated. He had the thin, spare look of so many of our people. We tried running a five-a-side football team for a while, but even those who enjoyed it soon found they just didn't have the stamina. Alec would talk to anyone, and tell them his convoluted life, involving appeals for justice from both the courts and the allegedly wealthy family who had abandoned him. It may have been true once, before it got lost in the embellishments. He would walk off his nervous energy, traversing the city and back again, hoping to find the destination that never quite materialised. When you don't know where your home is, how can you find it?

HAVE YOU GOT ANYTHING FOR ME?

Every day we have difficult decisions to make. We don't always get it right.

I am about to drive home when I remember the bags of food kindly given me by St Saviour's the day before. I start to unload the boot when one of our customers happens to notice. Being on your uppers makes you keenly observant.

Have you got anything for me? The old question is at once hopeful and used to disappointment. I'm supposed to add food to the general collection inside the Crypt of food generously given. But this man is in need. No one asks for food unless they need it; the resale value of tinned baked beans is not high on the street. I give him a bagful, and he is delighted. But one or two others have noticed, and begin to ask the same question. I tell them it needs to go inside, and suggest they ask at the front desk. They turn away, disappointed. I am disappointed myself. Should I have given more out? Or none at all? We try to identify those most in need, and make sure donations go where they can do most good; but sometimes spontaneity takes over. This time, it may make our friend the object of envy, and provoke resentment.

Such a little thing. I knew they had all just had a good lunch from us. But I know where my next meal's coming from; they don't.

NIGHTS

The Crypt is open 24/7. During the day it is very active; filled with busy staff and – in normal times at least – over a hundred people who come to us for help. We do what we can. I have often known colleagues come in on their day off because they felt it was necessary; someone needed more help. Evenings and nights are different. Sometimes people feel more able to talk in the hours of darkness; often they sleep badly and roam around, physically and mentally.

Debbie works nights. Those who work the night shift at the Crypt have my utmost respect; often one woman looking after thirty or more unpredictable men, some of them addicts, some mentally unstable. These days we have someone on security as well. But it's still a hard job. This week has been particularly difficult. One of our young women residents is cunning and manipulative: maybe she has had to be to survive. However, this is further complicated by her regularly using a potent mixture of heroin and crack cocaine; five of each, which is quite a lot. Regrettably, this makes her hear voices – or makes those voices louder. They tell her to do unfortunate things like urinating in her room, propositioning others, and constantly demanding attention from staff, all through the night. This has been very wearing for everyone; to her fellow residents as much as to our staff.

During the daytime she is mostly asleep in her room, or comes out to further manipulate people, at which she is very skilled.

She is due to move on. In every way, we trust. And soon, please God.

THE OTHER TWO

W*ho prays for you? Who prays for the priest?* Robbie looks
at me earnestly. I tell him that I know myself, and all
our work here, to be surrounded by prayer. It's the first thing
I ask for, when people ask what they can do to help. Because
we cannot do this work in our own strength. *Can I pray for
you?* And he lays his hand on my shoulder, and from the midst
of his own troubled circumstances, he prays for me, and gives
thanks for all the blessings of this life. This giving thanks is itself
a miracle of blessing; Robbie lost his wife three years ago. His
friend supplied her with the drugs she had managed to give up;
they both overdosed and died. Robbie's first reaction was to
lose himself in the same drugs; to numb the pain; to get out of
this life for a little time; to forget. But it wasn't the answer, and
he knew it. Eventually he found his way into rehab, and they
helped him turn his life around. When he left, he came back
to the Crypt.

And this morning, he asked to talk to me. Not to tell me
his troubles; rather, he wanted to thank God because his life
has changed. He doesn't have a job; his relationship with his
family is still fragile; he is living in a shared house with other
recovering addicts. And he is thankful for it all.

We mostly take things for granted: the gift of life itself;
our health and strength; the gifts of sight and hearing; having
enough to eat; somewhere safe and comfortable to sleep.

Some people have suffered so much they curse God. Some
people have suffered so much they thank God. It can go either
way. The other two crucified with Jesus show us that.

STILL HERE

It was Christmas. I was sleeping up in Miggy woods. And I thought to myself I might as well just end it all now. Last year I'd had family and kids round me. Now there's nothing. And that's what I was thinking when I walked into town. That I'd kill myself that night.

As Mel tells me his story, his eyes go far away; in his mind he's back there, in that place of absolute despair. We started talking about this because we have just lost someone to suicide. I would not wish it on anyone, but it helps that I have come very close to the same thing three times in my life. I have stood alone on the same high bridge.

So Mel came into town that Christmas. He was sat begging on Boar Lane when a teenage girl, with her dad looking after her, came up to him. She had decided to give her Christmas money to people who were homeless; so she was going round the streets, giving to everyone she found begging, until all her money was gone.

She would never know the difference that made, in Mel's case at least. Yes, he was glad of the money; but it was more than that. It was simply the sense that someone cared; that his life wasn't worthless. *That's when I started to hope again. That things might get better. So I didn't finish it that day. And I'm still here.*

REFERRING

I'm going to see my daughter today. This is often a big thing in the lives of our people. Frequently what brings someone to us is a final breakdown in relationships. They only come to the Crypt when there is nowhere left to go. The guilt and regret of having lost everything, including the love of those who were closest, is unbearable. So I am glad that our friend is going to see his daughter. *How long is it since you've seen her?* Sometimes it takes years to heal a broken past; court-orders may deny access, often for good reason. But it is hard.

I saw her six months ago. He still looks troubled, apprehensive. *How old is she?*

Don't know. Difficult to say. This is unusual. People usually remember their children's birthdays, even when all else has been obliterated. But maybe he has never known her well – or maybe he has only learned of her existence recently. Sometimes adult children arrive in our people's lives without their existence having even been suspected. This is normally a joyful thing.

I got referred to her by my GP.

Sorry, who?

My doctor. Ah. Not daughter then. *No! Course not. I haven't got a daughter.*

Maybe I need to wear my hearing aid more regularly. I was prescribed it last year, but only normally wear it for Church, where I can turn it to T to hear the sermon easily, and turn it off in cases of heresy or boredom. It would be heretical to suggest the Almighty does the same. We are all, after all, his much-loved daughters and sons. (And doctors.)

CHOSEN

One of my friends taps my clerical collar and says *I want one of those*. I tell him, as I have before, that he needs to belong to a Church first. Because that's who ordains you. No one gets ordained in the abstract; you get ordained to serve, and you don't always get to choose who. He tells me – again – that Jesus didn't need all that learning stuff, he just did it. And I point out, perhaps unfairly, that Jesus had studied the Scriptures well enough to be able to beat the scribes and Pharisees at their own game; he knew the learned tradition inside-out.

But I just want to serve Jesus.

You are doing.

Yeah. But I want one of those collars.

Before ordination, I wanted to be able to preach to people and encourage them to find God. Some years later, I wanted to tell my congregation that God was to be found everywhere, not just in church.

Jesus chose his disciples very carefully; he commissioned an international HR company, set up a website, interviewed thousands of hopefuls, got down to a short-list and then, after extensive psychometric testing, chose his twelve. You'd need to do all that if you were planning to change the universe. Actually, he asked a couple of probably illiterate fishermen, walked on a bit round the shore, and asked a couple more. Somehow it worked. Well, almost. There's always Judas, the treasurer. Bishop Inge once asked some children what they thought Jesus was doing when, as the creed tells us, *He descended into hell.* There was a pause, before one of them answered: *I think he was looking for his friend Judas.*

SOCIALLY DISTANT

During the COVID Lockdown, it was hard not being able to sit across the table from our residents. Sharing a meal together levels the playing field. Jesus did it a lot. This lunchtime, seeing our friends sat at separate tables, spaced widely as though they were sitting an exam, I wander rather aimlessly around. One of them calls me over. Mary wants to arrange a talk. Gladly. I will come and find her after lunch.

We meet up in the foyer, socially distanced. Her make-up is so bright orange she looks like an Oompa-Loompa. But Mary is doing her best to look pretty. She tells me she comes from a Traveller background. She tells me about her children, about her addictions, about her partner who beat her up badly a week ago. Then I understand; the make-up hides the bruises. *It was terrifying: I didn't know why he was doing it.* There had clearly been other times when she did know; when like so many victims of domestic abuse she believed she deserved it. Lord, have mercy. She wants to go to Mass. During the pandemic, she needs a ticket. I arrange to get her one, and give her a blessing and a rosary. Did she make it to Mass? I don't know; by Sunday she had gone from us. Maybe somewhere better. *Jesu mercy, Mary pray.*

ON THE ROAD

It was the morning of the Crypt's ninetieth birthday; 14th October 2020. In the middle of the Coronavirus pandemic, we had not planned anything in particular. We gathered for Morning Prayer, seated at distanced tables in the Assisi Café. We said again the familiar words:

This is the day that the Lord has made: Let us rejoice and be glad in it.

Truly, we have cause to rejoice: not that our work is still needed; not that homelessness is at least as great a curse as it

was ninety years ago; but that we have been given the vision to help those who come to us, and the means to provide that help.

We read together something written by our founder, Don Robins. It spoke to our condition, now as then.

Then I was able to read a message from Don's son Ian, which had arrived – as one of the small miracles which surround our shared life together – just that morning.

Blessings on all you are doing – and love and blessings to all the team there. Then Ian recalled my own account of giving money – which we never do – when I had first started at the Crypt. He told us a story from his father:

A request for money to go and visit a dying mother in Scotland met with great sympathy – the chap was taken to Leeds station, a ticket purchased and he was put on the train, and waved to as the train departed. There were no further requests!!

The call to be as gentle as doves and cunning as serpents was necessary then as now. That morning we laughed together, then wept together on hearing of the death of one of our former residents, Danny; who himself had a mother in Scotland, who will now be mourning the death of her son, too young.

The old Scots song 'Loch Lomond' also has a story to it. It is said that two brothers were imprisoned by the English. The elder was condemned to death. The younger was to be released, but asked if he could give his life instead, since his brother had a wife and children. His request was granted. The High Road is the one we take through this life; the Low Road leads to the grave: *And I'll be in Scotland afore ye.*

Danny's is the third death we know of this week; two to suicide, one of them found by one of my colleagues. This has gone on since the Crypt first opened. By the grace of God, we continue to be here to try to answer whatever need comes to us, and to try to help our people as they journey on the rough High Road. Sometimes they make it to heaven before us.

MIRACLE

Poor Joel is troubled. Actually he's troubled in every aspect of his life, but this is a specific trouble. He's just got a new place to live: a room in a shared house; one of the old Victorian terraces in the student area. What troubles him now is that he has heard that his room lay empty for a year; Joel's mind tends towards the dark side, and he has become convinced that someone died there. *Things have been moving round.* Given the amount of alcohol that he drinks every day, it would be more surprising if things had been keeping still, but let it pass.

I say I will come with my colleague Felicity, whom he trusts, and bless his new place. Once there, I tell him that it's an area I knew well as a student, hoping to make it seem comfortingly familiar. From the window of his attic room, we see the arts centre which was the old St Margaret's church. Then we look up. There is a most beautiful, unusual sky. Joel takes a picture of it on his mobile. I tell him it's what's called a mackerel sky; a sign that the weather is going to change. We pray that indeed it may be a sign for him that his life is going to change. God knows he needs it.

We pray for his bedsit, for light and life, and give him a crucifix, which he puts on the only shelf of his barely furnished new home.

We talk a while more. As I leave, praying again for his blessing, he says, *I won't forget this. Specially that Miracle Sky.*

Mackerel or miracle, it's all good.

MAYBE TOMORROW

I drop my empty coffee mug into the kitchen, by the sink. This gives me the chance to see how our wonderful cooks and washers-up are doing. Today there was only Algie, whose whole demeanour is suspicious, as though the whole world is against him. Knowing that he wouldn't welcome anything more, I give him the minimalist Northern Male greeting: *All right?* He grunts, barely. I have hardly stepped back into the corridor before he comes suddenly out: *Vicar?* (We answer to anything vaguely clerical; no one has yet addressed me as *Vicarage,* though I live in hope). *Can I have a blessing?* I wonder what has happened to this poor man, to bring him out of his desperately protected shell enough to be able to ask for help. *Gladly.* He stands, writhing uncomfortably. *Do you want a blessing for anything in particular?* Sometimes it helps to frame things; to drill down to one particular thing, when the whole of life feels like a mess. *Just to keep going on. I want protecting.* He is struggling. Trying to hold it all together when it is all falling apart. I begin to pray, and put

 my hands on his shoulders. He tenses. For too many of our people, touch is painful. *Noli me tangere.* As we pray, he relaxes. We pray for the blessing of God to surround him, to be a light for him in the darkness. *Be thou my guardian and my guide.* I haven't quite finished the traditional words of Trinitarian blessing when he says *Amen.* That's enough. Like a wounded animal coming for help, he can't take any more. Not now. Maybe tomorrow. He goes back to his kitchen, to lose himself in work again. Maybe tomorrow.

THAT IS, THIS NIGHT

It is Maundy Thursday. Together with Lighthouse, we are holding a service upstairs in St George's Church to remember all those who have died in the past year. Despite our fears at the start of the pandemic, none of our people have died from COVID. Other things have got to them first; overdose, suicide, murder, or bodies that have just given up after years of neglect. Lisa helps me put the list together, and in doing so breaks down on hearing that David has died. She didn't know. He had talked to her; told her how his partner had thrown herself off a bridge, ten years ago. He stayed living in the same council flat because there was nowhere else to go. That meant he had to cross that same bridge every day. The constant daily reminder got too much for him; one day he just walked out. He was not entitled to another council flat because he had intentionally made himself homeless.

He came to the Crypt, and eventually talked to Lisa. After a little while he left us, but no one seemed to know where he'd gone. Sometimes that's how it happens; people appear out of nowhere, and disappear back into it. Someone heard that he'd died, and his name got added to the list. And that's how Lisa found out. She was angry; and hurt; and grieving for another of our friends who might have been helped, but wasn't. Angry because the system had failed him; hurt because she cares.

The liturgy for this day includes four extra words: *Who on the night he was betrayed* – **that is, this night** – *took bread and gave you thanks* …. Our friend David too had been betrayed. We give thanks for his life, and commend his wounded soul to God. Who loves, who heals.

THE SACRAMENT OF CHOCOLATE

Easter approaches. The commercial world hasn't quite (yet) managed to turn the Glorious Resurrection into the annual feast of avarice and gluttony which now marks the Nativity of our Lord. Our generous donors have given us lots of Easter eggs and chocolate. Lisa takes great care to make sure that everyone has an egg, topped off with a fluffy yellow chick to make them smile. Chocolate is important to the Crypt. It's a sign of luxury; of that which is not necessary but much appreciated. The good food we serve is a necessity; our talented chefs can make a special meal out of anything we get given.

Sometimes, when it all gets too much, I go in and see the boss, whose door is genuinely – and literally – always open. Sometimes I break down. We all do. He gives us chocolate, because chocolate keeps the dementors away. And I wipe my eyes, and pull myself together, and say, *The day it stops getting to me is the day I need to stop doing this job.* He understands. We can only do it by being vulnerable. By needing the unnecessary things like chocolate. Like wine. That's the sacramental bit; He comes to us in bread, which is a necessity; and in wine, which isn't. We don't need both; but our Lord gives himself in both. The twin signs of that which sustains life; food and celebration.

Does that make chocolate a sacrament? In the end, everything is.

MARY

One of our young women residents has asked to see me. Younger women especially are extremely vulnerable when staying with us. We do our best to protect them. I go to visit her after lunch, and find her in the corridor, on her way out with a friend; both made up to the nines, and in short skirts, though it is midwinter. She tells me it is her birthday; her first since her dad died, and she misses him. She is 26 today; about the same age as my own dear daughter. She tells me about her dad; how he wasn't always around when she was growing up, but whenever he did visit he brought her something; sweets or jewellery.

And now, on her birthday, he wasn't here for her. We pray for him, commending him to the infinite love of God, who made him, who loves him, that all his hurt may be healed. As we pray, she starts to weep; for her absent father, and I guess for what her life has become. I give her a necklace with a cross, and pray God's blessing on her and her friend. Then they go off to work the streets.

I pray for them again, and for the men who will use them and discard them. These, too, are our daughters; and those who use them our sons. After they have gone, I too break down. Dear Jesus, who loved Mary Magdalene, let them know your love, and hear you call their name, and find their way safe home.

FIRST AND LAST

Dougal sat down on the Physio's bench and said, *I'm suicidal.* The first thing someone says is important. It's what's been knocking around in their mind; either they've prepared it, or – more likely if someone trusts you – it's just forced its way to the top.

Dr Phil, our wonderful physio, does more than fix damaged bodies; by careful attention and grace she heals wounded spirits as well. Dougal was in trouble when he came to us. He had assaulted his girlfriend because of jealousy. She had looked at someone the wrong way. Our people are often so emotionally fragile that a look is all it takes. We look after both victims and perpetrators, whoever comes through our doors. Now he was overcome with guilt; a shame so intolerable that death looked the better option.

Phil cared for him, listening deeply and talking gently as she worked on his shoulder.

He left her feeling better. When he came back a week later, the improvement was noticeable; not just in the body: his spirit had lifted and lightened. After a couple of weeks with us, he moved into one of our houses, finding encouragement with other recovering addicts. Over many hard months, he admitted his addictions; faced his fears; tried to make amends; acknowledged his powerlessness. For any of us this is hard; we want to pretend we are in control. From the depths of addiction this letting go takes unimaginable courage. A year or so later he was able to move out and move on; he started a gardening business. May his new life be a blessing to him; may his new growth flourish.

WITH US

We welcome anyone to the Crypt; but we ask people who are drunk or high to come back in a little while, because even one person off their head makes life difficult for the rest of our guests, who have come to us to find a safe haven. Their lives are difficult enough already.

Sometimes people manage to get through the net; our night staff are busy, and sometimes compassion overrules good order. It is meant to. But one night, one of our friends came in, and made his was unsteadily to where nine men were already asleep. Once there, he urinated on one of the beds. Unfortunately there was someone in it at the time. This caused a bit of an uproar, and it took a good hour or more to ask our friend to go away and sober up; to clear up the mess, to disinfect, to make up a clean bed, calm everyone down and turn the lights out.

When our friend came back a few weeks later, he greeted me cheerily.

Hey Rog, you know that night?

I remember it well.

When I pissed on his bed 'cause I were drunk, right?

Mm-mh?

It wasn't that. I've never liked him.

In the middle of the shared crazy laughter, I tried to suggest that there might be better ways of showing that you don't like someone.

We share the crazy laughter every day. We share the tears. That's what the Incarnation means. It's not about God being good and holy (though He is): it's not about a Jesus who is all love and compassion and forgiveness (though He is). Emmanuel means *God with us.*

UNTIMELY FROST

P ete came back to Leeds after ten years living rough on the streets of Manchester. He learned to stuff newspaper down his trousers and up his sleeves to keep just a degree or two warmer in winter. He reckons that that degree or two saved his life more than once. He helped me understand. One of the questions alcoholics don't get asked is why they drink. The answer, if you give someone time to answer, and if they are generous enough to trust you – generous in spite of all the times they've been ignored, bad-mouthed and rejected as worthless – the answer is often that they drink to numb the pain. To get out of the present for a little while, because it hurts too much.

That is why Ella took drugs. Her mother had committed suicide, and Ella had lost a baby in infancy. Then her surviving son, struggling to cope with his own emerging sexuality, took his own life. She and her partner Mick scored some heroin one night, at a time when it was commonly being laced with Fentanyl, increasing its potency a hundredfold. Mick collapsed, and was pronounced dead in the ambulance. Unable to cope without him, with yet another death, Ella deliberately took an overdose, and died. Had she but known, Mick was successfully resuscitated. The echoes of *Romeo and Juliet* horrified us all. Mick was distraught. Normally, anyone found to be using, whilst living at our dry house, would be given notice to leave. That's the agreement. But in these circumstances, he stayed with us, and we stayed with him. The process of recovery meant facing the pain. We do what we can to share it, to ease the intolerable burden. He is managing. Just.

HIM UPSTAIRS

Maisie had had an interesting life. Most people have, but only tell you the good bits. Our people often tell it like it is; at rock bottom there is little to be gained by dissembling. Maisie was an orphan, and grew up cared for by nuns somewhere down south fifty-odd years ago. She had never lost her East End twang. Her memory of the nuns was that they were kind, thank God. Certainly she had a strong faith, and would affirm this every time we met; *I don't care what you are – black, white or whatever – Him Upstairs looks after us all!* Then she would tell me that she was having an operation next week. A hip replacement. I would wish her well, and promise to pray for her operation and recovery. The next week she would be back with us, and tell me again that she was having a hip replacement next week. Like tomorrow, next week never came.

Then she just disappeared; or at least stopped coming to the Crypt. This happens. Sometimes with men, it means they've got sent down for a long spell; less frequently with women, and almost never with a woman of Maisie's age. No one seemed to know where she'd gone. Our people's lives are often lived alone; self-sufficient, just.

This all happened a couple of years ago. We pray for her sometimes, and for all those who have come to us for a time and then vanished. We can't do any more for them than that. But we trust. *Him Upstairs looks after us all.*

MASK

Preparing for morning prayer in the Assisi Café, I had opened the doors of the triptych, and appreciated again Steve Simpson's wonderful miniatures of the paintings in our chapel; the apostles gathered round the Last Supper, each one a portrait of one of our residents at the time. The painting of Jesus isn't immediately recognizable as anyone, but is a mixture of different people: in artistic terms, Jesus is a composite. (Discuss.)

I was due that afternoon to go for my first anti-COVID vaccination, and was feeling slightly guilty about it, knowing that so many others had not yet had it. Then one of our lesser-known clients came in, and engaged me in a rambling stream of conversation that clearly owed most of its content to whatever narcotic he had just enjoyed. He insisted on coming to within a few inches of my face; as I stepped backwards, so he stepped forwards, and intensified his ramble. This little dance was repeated; by the time we reached the back wall the others had noticed, and told him he needed a mask.

I don't need a mask. I've been given immunity by God.

I was about to point out that if he had, I hadn't, when a couple of the lads came up and very efficiently marched him away. I didn't feel too bad about having the injection after that.

After morning prayer, Arja made an announcement. She began, *Jesus isn't here today.* At least, that's what I thought she said. It's not always easy to hear people from behind a mask. On reflection, I think she said *Peter.* Not Jesus then, who we hope is always here, composite or not. His presence isn't obvious; he often wears a mask.

GROWING UP

It may be true, as Dora Gurney wrote, that *one is nearer God's heart in a garden than anywhere else on earth.* Unless one is a serpent in Eden perhaps.

We called our recovery initiative *Growing Rooms* for a reason. It provides somewhere safe for people to live, and to grow well and strong. Along the way, a lot of our people develop a taste for growing things rather than smoking them. Planting seeds, tending them, seeing the first shoots appear, delighting in visible growth; all heals the spirit. Or as one of our lads put it, *It does something to your head.*

Then one of them tells me about recovery. They have some good advice; for the first year grow a plant. If that survives, get a dog. After another year, if the plant and the dog survive, you might just be ready for a new relationship with another human. By then you have learned to care for something besides yourself.

Maybe that's why it can hit them hard when a plant dies; it's just another sign of failed hope. Waiting before beginning a new relationship is both wise and difficult. All the temptation is there to lose yourself in someone new. It's wonderful, feeling loved; it is the very thing so many of our people consistently lacked.

But recovery from any trauma – addiction, illness, bereavement – takes time to heal before you regain equilibrium, and come back to yourself. Never quite the same; hopefully better, given the right conditions. Waiting a little gives you time to grow straight again; to know yourself better. Watching things (and people) grow helps. It does something to your head.

> *All that we need to do, be we low or high,*
> *Is to see that we grow nearer the sky.*

YET

The council asked us to take Jessie in yesterday. We refused. She had recently been staying with us for a month before moving on into a flat. A week later she was evicted. She had been violent and abusive to the neighbours, manipulative of staff, and destructive of property; much as she had been when staying with us. She had made life hell for our other residents, and refused any help offered to her. All this is undoubtedly due to her long-term mental conditions, poorly managed. Amongst other things.

The really hard part is looking after a lot of people at the same time. It's like having children; where you have more than one, eventually they fall out and deliberately hurt each other. The best you can do is to protect the weak, correct the other, and let them know they are constantly loved. Or something like that. If we had just the one client, even that would be hard: we can't heal someone's whole life overnight. God can, but seems to like a bit of co-operation on their part.

Over the whole charity, we are looking after a hundred people at a time. This is only possible by the grace of God, who also turned people away; from Eden, from the banquet they didn't come to; from the wedding because they weren't ready for it. Their choice.

Sometimes that's how it is with our people; they're not ready for it. Yet. Always *Yet*. Maybe next time.

Nonetheless, we are appalled at turning Jessie away, because that's not what we do. But there are a few – very few, but some – whose needs are so extreme, so complex, so multiple, that they need more specialised help than we can give. If we say no, they might just get it. As one of my colleagues said, *We don't do open-heart surgery either.*

TRYING

Jez came to the back door wanting his e-cig charging. He has technically made himself homeless – again – after leaving one of the least secure parts of Leeds, where allegedly a drug-dealer kept coming into his flat, vaguely threatening. He needs to make a formal complaint to the police in order for Housing Options to consider him eligible for re-housing; but the nature of the threat is unclear and unsubstantiated. We will see him again. I take his e-cig for charging, and suggest he comes back in an hour.

An hour or so later, Chris comes to ask me if I have told someone to come back this afternoon for some food. I am able to reply with unusual clarity that I have given no such instructions to anyone. We discover that it is our friend Jez, who has already had a substantial lunch of sausage cassoulet with us, and is just trying it on. We try to make best use of the limited resources we have; and, incidentally, to encourage honesty, which helps us meet their needs. There is clearly more to his story than he is telling us. If he had just asked for more food, I would in all probability have said yes and found him a sandwich. As it is, I give him his charged e-cig, and send him on his way, not necessarily rejoicing, poor lad. He is known to be especially miserable, and doesn't really do rejoicing. Yet.

SCANDALOUS

Today is the Annunciation. We read the story of an angel coming to Mary; I asked what they thought it must have been like for her. One of the lads put it succinctly: *Well it must have scared the shit out of her.* Indeed. Our guys tell it like it is; like it is for them.

Their lives might be more courteously presented in the language of 1611 (the last good book to be written by a committee of 47) but would lose something in the translation:

For behold! An wayfarer cometh down from Osmondthorpe whose name was Kyle, which was sorely possessed by diverse substances and given unto much liquor, to the decay of his fleshly being, and the great annoyance of all they that had to do with him. And this same approacheth unto the Crypte with these words saying, "I would abide with thee this night, for verily have I naught whereon to lay my head, nor yet sustenance, and am anhungered and in sore travail." And straightway did the saints take pity upon him, and dresseth his wounds and feedeth him, and bade him tarry with them to the healing of his sorrows, which yet he did, and was thereafter delivered up unto the council upon the morn, and was enhoused to the great comfort of his soule and the relief even of his necessities. Selah.

Yea, verily. But even one so-called modern translation of the Scriptures has Gabriel salute Mary with the words, *Greetings, favoured one!* which would certainly surprise most of our residents at breakfast.

Our people do not lack understanding, and frequently bring fresh insights borne of lived experience to the timeless narratives of grace and redemption, and translate them into

124

their own lives. Sometimes people get offended by how they put it.

And I guess the good people of Nazareth did the same, in that biblical equivalent of a Northern pit village. *Can anything good come from Nazareth?* Substitute your own despised place; looked down on; scorned; the butt of jokes. As rare as a virgin in Nazareth. That's God's hometown. Our Lord might have been born down south, but if Peter had a northern accent, Jesus probably did too. Theologians call it *the scandal of particularity.* Sithee.

BALANCED

Having someone fall over in the corridor of the Crypt is not that unusual. This is less common when it happens to the chaplain. (Being unbalanced is probably a job requirement.) Despite rumours to the contrary, I was quite sober. We use non-alcoholic wine for the Sacrament, clearly labelled in case anyone is tempted to nick it. Frankly, you'd have to be pretty hard-pressed to enjoy the average Plonco Sacro, but then some of our friends are desperate enough to try drinking hand-sanitizer, which is why ours is not spirit-based. But my falling over became more frequent. Provisionally diagnosed with a form of Ménière's Disease which would only get worse, I was off work, unable to turn my head without the room spinning round. My colleagues visited me, and prayed for me.

At the end of nine months, I had an appointment with an audiologist. I shuffled in like an old man, leaning on a stick. She listened intently, then suggested a different diagnosis of BPPV.

She offered to try an Epley Manoeuvre, which took at most ten minutes. At the end of this I stood up, and turned round twice without falling over. The vertigo had gone completely. I walked out of the surgery twirling my walking stick like Charlie Chaplin. The Crypt is next door to the hospital. I walked in, and said I had been healed by a miracle. I was not the only one in tears. Yes, it was medically explicable; but I had walked into the surgery with a deteriorating life-long condition, and walked out cured. Miracles are also available on the NHS, at the hands of skilled and dedicated practitioners. God works in mysterious ways, some of which we understand. Hallelujah either way.

I'll have to find another excuse for falling over.

REAL

Take any words you've just prayed, and try addressing those same words to another human being. The stiltedness will probably make you laugh. Then take something you've just said to someone else, and try saying it as a prayer to God. If one or the other doesn't work, then we need to get real.

That said, I like liturgy. (Believing irreconcilable things is half the fun of faith). I love prayers that have been worn smooth over time; they make us one with the myriad generations gone before.

But some set prayer sounds like poetry that has aged badly and wasn't very good to start with. To the unchurched it can sound like the language of a contract or a courtroom. I remember in one service hearing a perplexed child say, *What's the judge doing now?*

I usually ask, at the beginning of our morning prayer together, if we know of anyone in particular need of prayer. Frequently our people will ask for prayer for family or friends, or enemies. Any prayer is good, probably. Or rather, anything which facilitates a personal relationship with God. We are encouraged to get people to ask Jesus into their lives; we ask their lives into Jesus. To let them see how God has been in their lives all along, even when it didn't feel like it. Maybe especially then. Recognizing this heals; it heals memories, and enables forgiveness of ourselves and of others, which surprisingly often feels the same. Welcoming whatever we are being given, moment by moment, heals and teaches us to *put on the mind of Christ,* to look through his eyes and see this infinitely beautiful world; broken and lovely.

Maybe God wants to be addressed in a very special way, but I doubt it. Jesus calls him Daddy. We don't need to tread carefully. God's not a grumpy uncle.

CALL COLLECT
6.6.8.6.

Lord, teach us how to pray.
Not what for once, but how.
Is it odd being called just God,
Or wouldst thou rather, Father?

And should we ask the prayers
Of interceding saints,
Or straight cut out the middle man,
And wholesale make our plaints?

Can it be He or She
To whom fly endless verses;
Sing we to you or thee
Unnumbered hymns or heresies?

Clad in sublimest prose,
The Second Person singular
Linguistically arose
In consubstantiate formula.

Courtly circumlocutions
To charm His Grace don't matter:
The Spirit seals and forwards our
Addresses, not the letter.

BUTTERFLY

I'm happy. Haven't been happy for a lot of years. Our friend's happiness is doubled by his recognizing it, and like all emotions it is contagious.

Happiness can slip away without our noticing it's gone, until one day we realize we have come to a flat plateau, a very long way down in the darkness. But even there, shafts of light break through, sometimes bringing unbearable regret for what has been lost.

For many of us, lockdown meant appreciating things we had taken for granted; sunlight, trees, flowers, birdsong, breath. I have watched our people notice all those things, and be thankful. The returning Spring is a sign of hope if we just stand still long enough to let it be so. You don't have to do anything, or be anything, except thankful. Our problem for the most part, whatever wicked lies advertising will tell you, is not that we haven't got enough; it is that we don't appreciate what we have.

One of the deep ironies of addiction is that what started as a pleasant thing makes people miserable; any pleasure over-indulged does the same. In the end, even the pleasure has gone. How it turns from something enjoyable into a strong monster is complicated. Trauma in childhood, feeling isolated, abandoned – worthless for whatever reason – all those can predispose to addiction. It comes from not being able to bear your life as it is.

Being brought back to the present can help; that's why mindfulness can work. Being in the moment frees us from shame for the past and fear for the future. Happiness is a very elusive butterfly if we chase it; keeping still reveals it everywhere. *The kingdom of heaven is within you.*

ANGEL

Stan has come to us from abroad. He got on the wrong side of a criminal gang, and is fleeing violence. He fears for his family left behind. He is young; maybe twenty. Yesterday he met a woman in the Crypt. His delight is evident, even in his broken English: *She just there for me. Sudden. Like angel.* They spent some time together; went for a walk, and listened to the birds singing in the park. *I was forget is Spring.* Then, suddenly anxious, he just left her and came back. He didn't know why. When you've lost so much, hope can be hard to accept. As he tells me all this, his face lightens, and he looks younger still. Now he wants to find her again, but isn't sure of her name; it was hard for him to pronounce. I suggest that one of the staff may know; many of our friends come regularly. Maybe we could get a note to her. His face clouds. *We could help you write it if you want.*

Our people have so much against them. Which of us, in Stan's circumstances, would have any idea what to do, how to cope, where to go? I often say to those close to despair, who need to recognize how well they have done, with all the odds stacked against them: *If I'd had your start in life, I wouldn't be doing half so well.* And always they are genuinely surprised. They don't think of themselves as heroes – far from it. But they are. Maybe not in the world's terms, who dismiss them as wasters, losers and scumbags. Just to keep going, day by day, takes courage and deserves encouragement.

Maybe she come tomorrow. Maybe she will. Angels do that.

SLIDING DOORS

One of our friends tells me of the time she was suicidal. Those of us who have come close to that can only recall it with horror. And maybe very great thankfulness that we didn't; that we're still here. Still doing what we can. Thankful that we never experienced a change of mind half-way down after we jumped.

Marie hadn't planned it. Standing on the edge of a railway platform she was overcome with despair, and was about to throw herself into the path of the train. At that moment a stranger came up and asked her what time it was. She told him. By then the train had passed; the moment had gone, and she went on to live. Only later did she realize that when he asked for the time, she had been standing under a clock. What prompted him to ask her? Did he sense something was wrong? Who was he? She never knew.

I remember a similar moment in my own life, having reached utter hopelessness, and about to end it all. Then someone offered me a cup of tea. Without pausing for thought, I said *Yeah, that'd be good. Thank you.* He never knew what the thanks were really for. Once the moment is passed, life has – by definition – got better. But the knowledge that it was possible haunts us. Everything that has happened to me since that moment forty years ago would never have been.

The best advice I know is this; in the moment when someone is suicidal, ask them something. Ask their advice. Ask them to help you. It gives them back to themselves for that moment; it shows them they are valued. After which the train has passed and the awful moment gone.

After that; other things. But in the crisis, ask *them* for help.

אמת

We talk in Morning Prayer about getting stoned to death, according to the Scriptures. The notion of getting *stoned* doesn't generally lead to the confusion it might, though it occasionally provokes a wry smile. Humour is never far away at the Crypt, thank God.

But today we are not talking drugs. We remember with sorrow and anger that people are still stoned to death in parts of the world, usually in the name of God. Christ, have mercy.

Then afterwards, one of our Growing Rooms lads tells me one of the stories of Prophet Mohammud which comforts him. He is not a Muslim, but has heard it from a friend who is, and remembered it. He tells me the hadith about the woman who walked a long distance to a well, to draw water for someone who needed it; and for that one selfless act all her many sins were forgiven. Of course those of us who have spent too much time with St Paul and Martin Luther would jump up and down and say we are not forgiven by good works. We are not forgiven by bad works either. And yet our works

– good, bad or indifferent – must mean something; they come out of love, or else mean nothing. And Jesus says *by their fruits shall ye know them.* In the end it's about relationship; our friendship with the Way, the Truth, the Life. Names don't matter. Aslan welcomes Emeth. Truly.

CYRENE

I just saw the back of two people walking down the corridor. I didn't know either of them, but could tell that one was a resident with us, the other probably a social worker; someone professional anyway. I knew because of the way they carried themselves. People come to us defeated, broken, and it shows even in how they walk. Being homeless means by definition being friendless; no one will take you home. No one wants you around. You have no job, no family who care enough, no purpose, no value. It's a miracle they're still walking at all.

In two weeks' time it will be Good Friday. Jesus stumbled. It gets forgotten that he couldn't bear it anymore. He needed help, and got it – maybe unwillingly – from a stranger, a foreigner.

We do what we can to share the burden, carry the cross, get our friends back on their feet again. This requires walking beside them, not striding out in front; not standing afar off and gesturing, but simply *being with*. As we do that, we find it's not as hard as it looked from a distance. We may even find that they are healing our burden, our griefs, as well. How? I don't know. Maybe Simon the Libyan found out. I just know it happens.

FAMILY HISTORY

A lot of our people don't know much about where they came from. They will probably know their mum, but even that is uncertain; too many of them were placed in care in childhood. From their accounts, *care* was a wildly optimistic word. Many suffered abuse, and are ashamed of it. They have no cause to feel shame – they were the victims – but that's what it does. Those dark memories, from the time when their characters were being formed, take a lifetime of enormous courage and unconditional love to overcome. Others might know their Nan, who was often the one constant in their lives. Many never knew their father; or only sporadically. Stepfathers vary; some people got lucky. Others had a lot of uncles who came and went.

Beyond that sketchy knowledge, few of our friends know much of their origins. They didn't hear stories of what it used to be like. This makes it harder. All they have to compare their lives with comes from what the rapacious media pushes at them now; rich and shallow celebrities, leading what are peddled as charmed lives.

It can be a comfort to know that Jesus' ancestry included quite a few spectacular villains.

History isn't just kings and battles. The everyday struggles of people just to survive can inspire us. Those of us who grew up hearing stories of courage in wartime, of unemployment, of unremitting toil in desperate conditions, of the struggle to find food to put on the table; for those memories and their inspiration we have cause to be thankful. Our forebears would think us incredibly wealthy.

Not a day goes by in the Crypt but that I am thankful for the love of my parents. That's what too many of our people never had. Which only unremitting love can heal.

READY OR NOT

Young Sam knocks on my door. He says he's got stomach-ache. Sadly, I cannot fulfil his request for some *Milk of Amnesia,* which would be a useful thing to have in many cases. He doesn't know what he should do. We go to find Christine, who will know what to do. As I thought, she tells him that if he's sick he must go home. But he has given his bus pass to someone else, apparently. It's a couple of miles walk up to Armley, where he is staying in one of our houses. After he's gone, one of the other lads volunteering in the kitchen says he's always going sick. He doesn't want to be here. *He's only here 'cos his mum told him he had to.* And there is the problem. We can only help those who want to be helped. The good intentions of others on their behalf don't count for much, unfortunately. The families of addicts suffer greatly, not least from guilt, often misplaced. Guilt is a wasted emotion unless it provokes change. Often people just get stuck in it.

Dorothy Parker was asked in a panel game to create a sentence using the word *horticulture.* She said, *You can lead a whore to culture but you can't make her think.* In my experience this is unfair to sex workers, who often think a lot, mostly with deep regret. In any case, as (probably) St Augustine said: *The Church is a whore, but she is still our mother.* Our friend Sam has every chance to turn his life round; but he only will when he's ready. My guess is that it won't be this time; but we always leave space for miracles. Maybe the next time, or the time after that, or the time after that. We can help him. When he's ready.

FRIEND

Andrew brings Isaac to see me. He is deeply troubled, poor lad. In the last few months both his parents have died. He was already estranged from his children. Now his partner has dumped him. That was the final straw that brought him to us. It usually is; people go through a series of crises, then their main relationship breaks down, they get kicked out, and come to us. This means that when they walk through our doors homelessness is just one of their problems. Isaac is broken.

His friend has brought him to me, to ask for a Bible. Certainly, he needs comfort, and hope; which in the end only comes from God. Everything else is a false distraction. By the time people come to us, a lot of the illusions have been stripped away.

I give him a paperback of Luke's gospel, and a Gideon Bible. Then ask if I can pray for him. Asking is at least a courtesy. Sometimes prayer is used to coerce or manipulate; a means of control. That is spiritual abuse. Jesus asked people what they want, so we ask the same. As often happens, in trying to frame his answer – going into the depths of his grief – Isaac breaks down. He has every appearance of being a hard man; useful in a fight: wiry and fast. Now he is weeping. He hides his face in his coat. Boys don't cry.

We pray for his healing and comfort; we pray for his children; we pray that his mam and dad may now be everything they were created to be. And we pray that he has the strength and hope to go on from moment to moment. And I thank God for his friend Andrew, who probably feels like the only friend he's got right now.

FEED MY SHEEP

Most of what we do at the Crypt is to care for those who come to us. There are, thank God, other charities whose work is to go out on the streets and look after those who are sleeping rough. We provide a safe place for them to come. But there are exceptions (always and everywhere; blessings have no rules). So Michael tells me something of his story. He was sleeping rough; *skippering* with another lad well known to us. They were sleeping on the church parapet which forms the roof of the Crypt. Even though this was autumn, and not the coldest time, it was cold enough – and years before agencies started giving out tents. In the days before the Crypt could accommodate more people, we used to give out sleeping bags to those who were sleeping rough. Only one a week per person was allowed. You had to hide it during the day. No matter how well you hid it, chances are it was gone by that night. So Michael spent every night on the parapet with his friend, having drunk themselves to sleep. And every morning, our Chief Executive would go up and wake them, and call them in for breakfast, and a shower and clean clothes if they wanted them.

Michael never forgot; more than the act itself, he remembered the loving kindness with which it was done, and knew that it was done in God's name. He held on to his faith. It was to be a long hard road, with many apparent conversions and successes, and as many failures, sliding back down into addiction, shame and crippling disappointment. It was going to one of the Betel rehabilitation houses, then coming through our own Growing Rooms, that made the difference. That and the love of God, served up as a hot breakfast, lovingly given.

IN-BETWEEN

Sometimes people come to us roaring drunk. We have found from experience that it is better for them (and certainly for our other friends) to go away and sober up (a bit). This is not always achievable. From time to time, someone will just lie down on the pavement outside the Crypt. Occasionally people see this and criticize us for our inhumanity. Often enough, we are not letting someone in because they have threatened violence against another of our residents. The duty of care is not clean and simple, however much we might wish it was.

Michael remembered one night on the pavement. When he woke up, he found there was a warm blanket over him. He had been too drunk and unpredictable to get let in; but he hadn't been abandoned. He woke in a pool of vomit, and found he had soiled himself. When morning came he was able to come in, get a shower, clean clothes and a hot meal. Until the next night.

For a while, Michael would go away from us. One of the worst times was when he was living in the most deprived area of Leeds. He worked in a cannabis factory in an old church building (high church, presumably). The irony got to him. It felt like a betrayal of his faith, feeding his addiction and others' in this once holy place. They got local children to bag it up.

As he tells me, his face turns dark at the memory. Shame haunts us. But even that, given to God, can be the means of healing. Nothing is lost. We are not who we were; nor yet everything we are meant to be, but something in-between.

Sometimes – usually even – it takes years to recover. Really recover. Some people don't make it, in this life. But some do. We are thankful.

SHAME INTERTWINES

Healing takes time. Sometimes it looks like a sudden miracle; but even that has been prepared for, in the long history of a lifetime; in the prayers of those we didn't even know were praying for us. Dick had been through the mill. His childhood had been so damaged he couldn't bring himself to speak of it. Like so many of our friends, he took drugs to numb the pain. He was gentle, and lost. He stayed in the Crypt for a while, then moved on to a flat which looked hopeful, but didn't work out. Back with us, a place came up in one of our shared houses. He took the chance gladly, and for some months all seemed to be going well.

Then, quite suddenly, he walked out. This happens sometimes; not always for obvious reasons. A few days later he was ready to talk about it. The reason was unexpected. Dick had discovered that one of his house-mates had stolen something from the Crypt. He was so angry at this betrayal of trust that he couldn't bear to stay in the same house, and left.

Anger shows itself in many ways. The worst is suicide, where – not always but sometimes – a rage which cannot be expressed is turned against yourself. This felt a bit like that. His anger took the form of punishing himself; he walked away from an unbearable conflict.

Only later did it come to light that he himself had also taken something from the Crypt that wasn't his. Once we knew, we could give him all the forgiveness he so desperately needed, and incidentally enable a reconciliation with his fellow offender.

We hold on to shame, hearing the voices of condemnation from childhood, when we were innocent and made to feel guilty. Constant forgiveness heals.

ARTHUR

I wondered about the big monochrome photo my colleague Martin kept above his desk. A grainy picture of a deeply weathered face, darkly pock-marked, with a rough beard and deep, gentle eyes. Eventually I heard his story. Arthur had come to us an inveterate alcoholic, and lived for some years in the old house on Regent Terrace; our Wet House for those who couldn't quite make it to our Dry House. The stories of the men there were always compelling; often tragic, told with courage and humour. Many of them had had more or less steady jobs and lives until the drink and some crisis pushed them over the edge. It was, as Martin said, *always a privilege to listen to them*. We did what we could to provide them with a safe community.

Arthur had been a miner until the pit was closed. That's where the pock-marks came from; the coal-dust never quite washed away. His photograph was so striking that we asked his permission to use it for the cover of *Entertaining Angels*. He was delighted, and agreed to be interviewed on camera. He spoke movingly of his life, the good times and the bad. Then he came to a halt. *I don't know why these people do so much for me*. He paused. *That's it*. We loved him, and he knew it.

In the years since, the old house – long past its best – has been demolished, and a new block of fifteen self-contained flats has been built, under Martin's oversight. The need has never gone away; Arthur was one of thousands who have come to the Crypt when there was nowhere else to turn. We have been able to help them, in the name of God. That is the answer to Arthur's question. He knows now. *That's it*.

SOCIETY

Gareth helped one of our people move on; Liam needed a telly and a fridge and an Xbox(the three vital signs of life). A refrigerator is admittedly pretty necessary now, especially if – like a lot of people – you rely on frozen ready-meals. What our friends call *ping meals:* straight from the freezer into the microwave: *ping!* If you live on your own, cooking from scratch can sort of lose its point. (And yes, in case you missed it, that was a confession). All the prophets had their particular sign. Jesus' sign was the shared meal.

Isolation and boredom destroy us. Not just the lack of stimulus, but a flat sense of purposelessness. Computer games can distract us; but so can porn and drugs. The real problem with pornography is that it dehumanizes; it separates the soul from the body – both ours and other people's. Advertising abuses this, so sexual exploitation is all around us constantly, stealing our senses to make money for someone else.

Unfortunately, Gareth's help wasn't enough. Liam wanted drugs more than white goods, and sold his fridge to Cash Converters. Then the Xbox, then the telly. Left with nothing, he just sat there; despaired, overdosed and died. It was a week before they found him.

In the end, we need some purpose; some reason to wake up; some contribution to make. For too many people Margaret Thatcher was right; for them, there is no such thing as society.

HOLY SMOKE

I try not to publicly criticize others for being greedy or selfish or proud. But I have often been criticized by other Christians because I smoke. I reply that it's important for me to keep one sin so I know what it's like for the rest of you. By way of encouragement, I have a small collection of photos of famous Christian smokers; C. S. Lewis, Pope John XXIII, Dietrich Bonhoeffer, the theologians Barth, Tillich and Niebuhr. It is easy to confuse the virtues of respectable society with the essential tenets of the faith.

Having a smoke with the lads has led to countless blessed conversations.

We are not supposed to give out cigarettes to our people, and generally I don't. But I think of another Leeds priest, the saintly Geoffrey Studdert Kennedy, who during the Great War became so known for dispensing prayer and cigarettes in the trenches that he was called Woodbine Willie. The most famous Baptist preacher, C. H. Sturgeon, believed that a cigar prepared his throat for preaching. When challenged, he replied that he would continue to *smoke to the glory of God*.

Of course it's bad for you. Very bad. But I was brought up in a tradition which counted smoking as sinful. So was drinking alcohol, wearing make-up (ladies, but presumably men as well), playing cards, going to the cinema, dancing, wearing brightly coloured clothes, travelling on a Sunday (well, frankly almost anything on a Sunday), and of course sex. This may have warped my conscience. It certainly warped a lot of people. Gluttony, usury, selfishness, hypocrisy and pride didn't get condemned as often: the sins of the world are more respectable.

It's a bit like those teachers who only mark the surface features – spelling, punctuation and grammar – and miss the lyrical creativity completely. That's easy to do. But it's more than that; the problem is that judgment often comes before compassion, or even observation. In a narrow faith, things are condemned not because they are bad for you, but because they are held to be sinful, if only because they give pleasure to the body. Once you go down that rabbit hole, there ain't no way back, save by the usual method, where we learn compassion through suffering.

But having agreed that one thing is allowable, where do we stop? Is mainlining heroin all right – or sniffing coke? One pint or eighteen?

Some people think you can't be a Christian and an addict. We have been led to believe otherwise in the Crypt. It was an addict who told me that *Jesus is the best*. He knew it.

In any case, something of the answer to all this is given in the story of two religious brothers; one a Franciscan, the other a Jesuit. They were debating one day whether smoking was compatible with prayer. Each agreed to ask his Superior. When next they met, the Jesuit asked how the Franciscan had got on. *No, sadly. He won't allow it.* The Jesuit smiled. *What did you ask him?*

I asked if it was permitted to smoke while praying. He said no.

Ah said the Jesuit, *I got a yes. I asked if it was permitted to pray while smoking.*

Don Robins, founder of the Crypt, wrote:

> A cup of tea, a talk, a smoke,
> An argument, the latest joke;
> So starts that fellowship of love,
> Which finds its end in God above.

INSHALLAH

Jordan asks me for a *rosemary*, but not prison-issue. He is about to be disappointed: those are the only rosaries I have; plastic, on a cord not strong enough to strangle yourself – or anyone else.

When you are beset by anxiety, the gentle rhythm of the rosary prayers can be healing. We are blessed by many traditions in the Crypt; Evangelical proclamations of Salvation; Pentecostal prayer in the Spirit; Catholic devotion; the Hebrew *Shema*. God is not limited; always *more than we can ask or think*. God loves us where we are. We try not to be so unsure of our convictions that we need to condemn everyone else's. We pray to be led into all truth.

Then Jordan tells me a story. A man dies and goes to heaven. The first person he meets is a radiantly beautiful woman, who welcomes him home. He asks who she is, then realizes: Mary, the mother of Jesus. He is overcome with sadness; *but I've not led a good life: why are you helping me?* Mary looks at him with deep compassion: *Do you remember going to Church once with your grandma when you were little? You prayed that day "Holy Mary… pray for us now and at the hour of our death". I never forget a single prayer.*

This makes me all the more sorry not to have the rosary he asks for. But he brightens up; *I can get a nice one for my sister.* That is a kind thought. Especially when he has next to nothing. I consider buying him a nice one; but then think better of it. It will help him to plan, save, and achieve such a kindness. And his sister will surely treasure it for what it is; a visible sign of love.

MONKEY

Roy had been with us for some weeks. People in wheelchairs are harder to house, requiring disabled access and special bathrooms. Despite his many problems, there was still more than a glimpse of the likely lad he had been in his youth. He told me he was from Hull, where I too had family; we talked of the pubs we both remembered. He was an enthusiastic drinker. One morning I found him, unhappy and tearful. *I want to go to a hospice.* We knew he was ill, but he was never forthcoming about his condition. We talked, and prayed. He brightened up a bit when I said we would contact St Gemma's, the wonderful hospice in north Leeds. They agreed to send out a team to assess his condition.

Most people who go into a hospice are assessed, looked after, get their medication sorted, and go home again.

Unfortunately, Roy was not ill enough to be admitted. Yet. For some weeks more, he stayed with us, alternately charming and driving us to distraction. As one of my colleagues put it, *He's a bit of a naughty monkey.* We have a few of those.

As his condition deteriorated, despite medical help, it became evident that he needed more than we could give him, and the hospice was called in again. This time, they agreed to take him. That's when the trouble started.

Most people want quiet and peaceful surroundings in which to approach the end of this life. But that had never been Roy's way. He wanted to carry on drinking, and smoking, and partying loudly with his friends. The hospice tried in every way to accommodate this, but it wasn't easy to reconcile all this with the prevailing ethos of calm and quiet needed by the rest of their patients.

After a couple of weeks of general mayhem, Roy walked out. He is still, I think, the only patient to have discharged himself from the hospice. He refused also to come back to the Crypt, and slept rough until he collapsed, was admitted to hospital, and died.

St Gemma's were, as ever, compassionate, and concerned that we hadn't together been able to meet his needs. I went up there, but first asked a couple of our people in the Crypt what they thought about hospices. *Hospice!* There was a moment's reflection. *Well, they're dead quiet aren't they.* For once I resisted the impulse to inappropriate laughter. *I mean, you need a bit of noise to let you know you're still alive!* I was able to relay these insights to the team at St Gemma's. Then we collapsed in laughter. They saw the point at once. The needs of our people are often different.

From that first meeting emerged a series of others, with dedicated and experienced staff considering what could be done. A research project was initiated, options considered and thought through. All of this has borne fruit; the hospice now provides regular nursing care within our flats in Hyde Park, where anyone approaching the end of life could stay and be cared for amongst the friends they know.

This is all Roy's memorial. We miss our naughty monkey.

TURNING

At Morning Prayer Chris asks us to pray for Mickey. I saw Mickey three days ago, and he was completely incoherent. When St Peter said the apostles couldn't be drunk because it was only nine o'clock in the morning, he'd clearly never been to the Crypt. We hope he's visited since. Truly, we are *surrounded by a host of witnesses*. The paintings in our lovely chapel depict the apostles, gathered around the table of the Last Supper; it is a reminder to us that the good meals we are able to provide are more than just earthly food.

We take comfort that the paintings are all portraits of our residents. We try to see the face of Jesus in whoever comes to us; and so these pictures are also portraits of our Lord. Heavily disguised, maybe; disappointed, angry, dishevelled, *men of sorrows and acquainted with grief*. All of humanity, just as they walk through our doors.

Today Mickey needs our prayers because he has had a fall; or jumped. He has broken his ankle. In hospital they discovered that he'd taken an overdose. He's not sure himself whether this was deliberate or not. Suicides don't want to die; they just don't want to live any more.

We hope – and pray – that this may be a turning point for him (rather than his ankle). Last week he wanted to go to rehab and get off the booze. The question was, did he want it enough to not drink? Often our people want someone else to do the heavy lifting. In the end we can offer advice, opportunity, the right environment; but you've got to want to do it yourself. This seems harsh. Especially when willpower is the very thing you lack. That's why AA talk about a Higher Power. Help comes when you admit you are helpless.

TODAY

I *'ve got my family back.* Billy tells me his story. It is always humbling to be so trusted. Many years ago, my psychiatrist told me that the most honest people he knew were recovering alcoholics. Those whose lives had been utterly broken; who know where rock bottom is and what it looks like. Addiction is a tornado; everyone close to it gets caught up in its destroying power. Families break apart; loved ones are hurt beyond measure. Billy tells me that because of his addictions his mother had not spoken to him for more than a year.

Now he tells me he has been clean of drugs for three weeks. That's the longest he's gone since he started using when he was fifteen, twenty years ago. His mum is thrilled, and hopes this can be a good example to his younger brothers, who are following the family tradition of addiction and crime. He tells me how much the Narcotics Anonymous meetings are helping; *for the moment.* There is an edge of fear in his voice. It is hard to have confidence in your own ability not to use again; there is a small persistent voice inside, nagging away and saying *You've never managed it before; why should this time be different? Who are you kidding?*

But that's all about tomorrow. That's why the twelve-step programmes all say *Just for today.* Not for tomorrow, or next year, or the rest of my life. I won't drink; just today. I won't use drugs; today. Whatever your addiction is, whatever virtue you aspire to, try it. Just for today.

ONCE

Barney tells me how much he appreciated this morning's gospel about turning the other cheek. His journey hasn't been easy; the usual toxic mixture of addiction and mental illness, over many years, the one feeding off the other. Now in his forties, he managed to stay clean of drugs for months, then something happened, and he went back to his old friend heroin.

So I had a relapse. He pauses, reliving the horror of it all. The disappointment and shame. The thought that he'd been fooling himself by thinking he could ever be different.

I felt cut off from God. He wasn't, of course. We never are; but it can feel like it; and after having once known that deep, compassionate, healing love, losing it is unbearable and terrifying.

I felt cut off from life. You feel like your spirit's drowning.

He didn't give up. He tried again. Now he's not used for over two years. That is like climbing a mountain in the darkness. He's done it. *I needed that relapse. Just to remind me how much I want to recover.* He gains strength from prayer; from the readings in *Just for today;* and from the gospels, as he did this morning.

We hear it so often, it's hard to remember quite how revolutionary this gospel is. Other people's take on it helps. I remember a story from prison. A big, strong man, the boss of the wing, became a Christian. Word got round, and it wasn't long before he was challenged by a weedy little runt of a man. *So you've become a Christian, right?* The big man nodded. *So if I smack you in the mouth you've got to turn the other cheek, right?* He nodded again, then answered with a single word: *Once.*

MARX OF FAITH

One of the lads tells me his grandad flew Lancasters during the war. I tell him about our founder, Don Robins, who flew with the Royal Flying Corps in WWI. He is impressed.

Blimey. They were just bathtubs with wings back then. I mean, the Marx brothers had only just invented flying.

I am more delighted than I can say by the thought of Harpo and Chico sketching out blueprints for their early flying machines. Sometimes remembering the Marx brothers helps us with our less immediately lovable clients:

You love your brother don't you?

No, but I'm used to him.

It's a start.

From everything we know, Don Robins would have appreciated all this. Saints laugh a lot; at the absurdity of this life, of all our hard-won certainties, or just for sheer delight. Laughter sometimes overtakes us when we are together in Chapel. It feels like a gift of the Spirit; a healing blessing on our work, bound up so closely with those whose lives have known every evil imaginable.

Certainly, one of the things always remembered about Don is his laughter. He had known great sorrow; the loss of comrades, the damage to those who survived. A determination to build a better world led him to ordained ministry, in a life of unremitting service. There are two sorts of martyrdom; the red and the green. Red martyrs are those who are murdered for their faith; Oscar Romero, Esther John, Janani Luwum: too many in our own time. Green martyrdom is different. Lives given wholly to service; caring lovingly for ageing parents; serving the poor of Calcutta; nursing those with COVID; or founding a charity which cares for the homeless and vulnerable of Leeds. We bless Don's memory every day: in the midst of tears; in crazy laughter.

SMASHING

My sage and experienced colleague Gareth tells me that we used to have a sliding door at the front entrance to the Crypt. Based on the model of a bank, apparently. But we quickly found out that our needs were different. Banks don't have disgruntled customers trying to smash the door down with bricks. Usually. But even that is some form of communication. Better they hit our door than another human being. It is perhaps part of what we are here for, however inconvenient.

I remember one vicar asking his congregation if they really wanted to engage with the local youth. They were enthusiastic. Then he said, *If they come, they will come as they are. They will smash windows, paint graffiti on the walls, and shout abuse at you. That's only some of what it will cost. But if we are to be there for them, that's part of who they are. We may be able to help. Now, are you ready?*

Our people get angry. Angry at the parents who betrayed their trust and gave them abuse instead of love. Angry at schools that couldn't cope with them. Angry at partners as damaged as themselves, who let them down, again and again. Angry at a society that gives them no purpose. Angry with themselves; crippled by guilt; trapped in a corner with no way out. All that is what smashes the doors down. We try to encourage a more articulate and productive conversation; but we sometimes have to get through the bad stuff first. Most people come round in the end; by the grace of God and a bit of encouragement. It can take years. That's all right; we've been here since 1930. God has all eternity.

BUILDING

It's like a morgue in here! It was indeed an unusually quiet morning in the Crypt. My thoughts went back to the original purpose of our building; it had for its first eighty years been a house of death, a burial chamber. It got cleared gradually from 1930 onwards, when the young vicar of St George's first opened part of it up as a refuge for wayfaring men. I knew one of the builders who had helped clear the rest of it in the 1950s.

Fred was only a teenager then, and found it difficult. Being a Yorkshireman, he just said *It wasn't very nice.* But he did it. And by his work, and the work of countless others over so many years, that house of darkness and death has become a place of light and life; of hope. We believe in the Resurrection; we also believe in life before death. We believe in giving everyone who comes to the Crypt the possibility of change; of new life; of hope that however dark things have been, it doesn't have to stay like that.

Many years later, when Fred himself was dying, he asked if I would conduct his funeral. He had been like a second father to me. I couldn't refuse. *Of course I will. It won't be easy.* He looked up at me from his hospital bed: *Nay lad, if I can do it you can.*

Just a couple of weeks later, I fulfilled my promise to him. It was – like all the best farewells – a mixture of tears and laughter. Tears for the much loved friend we had lost; laughter as we remembered him as he was; and that deep mixture of both which trusts that God our most loving father heals, and restores all that was meant to be, and wipes away every tear.

THANKFUL

Sometimes we get discouraged. The sheer enormity of the task; the unremitting demands; the endless stream of people needing help. That, generally and by grace, we cope with. What can be harder is coping with the failure of the system. Those working in social care often do their best with limited resources and staff, and are an easy target when something goes tragically wrong. But those who come to us for help have often been let down by the system; their appreciation helps us to keep going.

Not all my clerical colleagues agree, but I find that wearing a dog collar – even with just a bit of it showing – opens more doors than it closes. One of our newly arrived residents, whom I have not met before, approaches me in the corridor. *I just want to tell you. When I was in prison, I prayed to God to take me home. I felt so bad, like it couldn't get any worse. And I prayed that God would take me home. Then I got out, and he brought me here. So he's answered my prayer. I've never seen anywhere like this. Everyone looks after you. They're not here for themselves. Volunteers fall over themselves to do stuff. This place is blessed by the Spirit.*

All this I believe to be true. By grace alone. Sometimes it takes someone from outside to articulate it. Sometimes we need to be reminded to be thankful.

EPILOGUE

When I started as chaplain to St George's Crypt in 2013 we were providing lunch for 50-60 people a day. By 2019 that figure had doubled. In 2008 we thought fifteen rooms would be enough; ten years later we looked after more than fifty in the Crypt itself on a hard night.

During the pandemic of 2020 we were caring for 120 in alternative accommodation, as well as the 65 we regularly house across the whole charity. In that year alone we provided 14,972 bed spaces in safe and secure accommodation; 9289 at Regent Lodge, our supported accommodation for men who are dependent on alcohol, and 708 Homeless and Health Inclusion bed spaces in our city centre emergency accommodation.

Each of those statistics represents a much-loved child of God.

Whatever the long-term effects of COVID, we can be sure of one thing; the weakest in society will suffer most. Everyone who comes to us has their own story to tell; stories of courage in the face of crushing burdens, usually unacknowledged. We persist in believing that every one of those who comes to us is loved by God; deeply, personally. We try to show them that love; in practical help; by valuing each one who comes to us. The work is difficult, often frustrating, costly, and rewarding. We do what we can, by grace.

If you want to get involved, our website is easily found. If you live far away, simply search the internet for your own town and the word *homeless*. The need is everywhere.

We ask your prayers, without which none of this was ever possible.